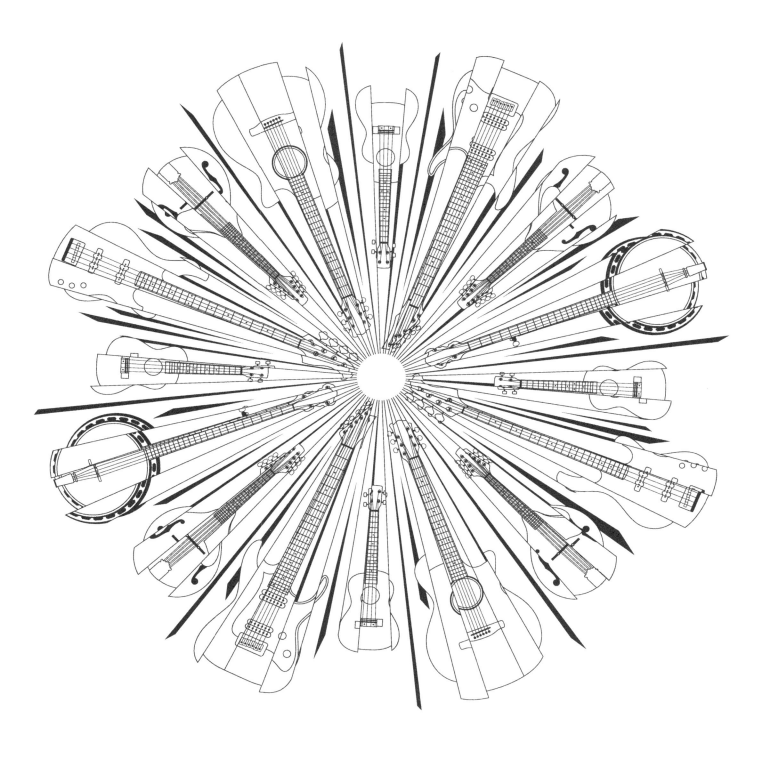

All of my books are dedicated to my wife Lisa and my daughters Abigail and Eloise Golden.

The Ultimate Guitar Arpeggios Book

Here are some of my favourite quotes from respected musicians. Hopefully they inspire you to practice as much as they did me!

'If you're struggling to play something fast it means you're not ready to play it fast. If you keep trying to play it at the speed that's beyond what you can actually do, you'll end up teaching yourself bad habits. The solution is to play it at a sensible speed and concentrate on playing the notes well.'

~ Guthrie Govan

'Notes and chords have become my second language and, more often than not, that vocabulary expresses what I feel when language fails me.'

~ Slash

'A lot of people think that if they learn to read music they are gonna lose their feel or their groove or something. It's the stupidest thing I have ever heard'

~ Frank Gambale

Scan the QR code below with your phone/tablet to get useful links to aid you with this book or visit www.karlgolden.org/GuitarBookLinks

www.karlgolden.com

ISBN: 979-8-63903-420-6

Contents

Introduction

As with all the books in The Ultimate Guitar Series, I wanted to create a bible of useful shapes that will help you unlock the fretboard. With this book we are looking at arpeggio shapes, starting from the most basic triad arpeggios to the more advanced extended arpeggios such as ninths, elevenths and thirteenths. So many arpeggio books I have read in the past have hundreds of unnecessary shapes that are just repeated in every key. This can be confusing and make players think they have a massive volume of arpeggio shapes to learn, which they don't.

Over my 20 years of playing guitar I have found that it is better to learn arpeggio shapes in one key that can then be moved anywhere on the fretboard, which is why I have heavily focused on the CAGED arpeggio shapes in this book. Don't feel like you have to learn them all, learn what you need to help improve your playing. Also, don't worry too much if you do not understand what the CAGED system is, I will give you a basic overview of it in this book. The most important thing to remember is where the root note is, then you can move whatever arpeggio shape you are learning to that position on the fretboard. Easy as pie!

In my teenage years I only associated arpeggios with sweep picking, I thought that was the hardest technique to learn on guitar, which to an extent is true if you want to play super-fast over all six strings and accurately! However, over the years I have discovered lots of other techniques and tricks to play arpeggios, not only in my improvising but also in my song-writing. I massively over looked the power of using arpeggios in my playing for years, which was a big mistake as they are so useful when improvising and following chords. You can't go wrong with an arpeggio as it follows all the notes in the chord. It is essentially a broken chord with each note being played separately rather than all together, meaning that each note will sound great when you improvise over that respective chord.

I have created lots of practice ideas in this book that incorporate a range of techniques such as alternate picking, legato, string skipping, tapping and sweep picking, to help you to play the different arpeggio shapes horizontally, vertically and even diagonally. With these different techniques I will show you how to play arpeggios on every combination of strings - including just one string patterns with the magic of tapping! With each pattern in this book I will demonstrate how to practice, whether it is using alternate picking or sweep picking. I also recommend checking out **'The Ultimate Guitar Sweep Picking Book'** if you are interested in diving deep into the world of sweeps and specialised shapes without barring.

To get the most from this book I highly recommend you learn where each note is on the fretboard, or at the very least on the low strings E, A and D. There is a full chart of every note of the fretboard in this book to help you. Learning all the notes on the neck will allow you to quickly identify the root note and move the arpeggio shape to that position. Every arpeggio shape in this book will show the root notes with a white circle and you will notice that all the arpeggio shapes are connected over the whole fretboard.

I hope you find this book as useful for your guitar playing as I have in making it. Head over to **www.karlgolden.org/BookDownloads** for the mp3 audio downloads for each of the exercises in this book. If you have any questions please feel free to contact me on my website at **www.karlgolden.org/ContactPage** or email me at **info@karlgolden.org**.

All the best,

KARL GOLDEN

How to Use This Book

For every arpeggio in this book there will be a number of guitar shape boxes, like the one you see below, that represent the fretboard of a guitar and the six strings (in standard tuning). These shapes are movable so you will not see any numbers on the frets. With regards to the formula of the arpeggios don't worry if you are not a master of music theory, I have laid out the guitar intervals in the key of D later in this book these are movable to whatever key you want and will help you see how these arpeggio shapes have been built. You can also visit **www.karlgolden.org/ReadingCharts** for a video lesson on reading guitar charts and for more essential video lessons visit **www.karlgolden.org/YouTube.**

Below is an example of a Major 9 arpeggio chart to show you how to read them in this book:

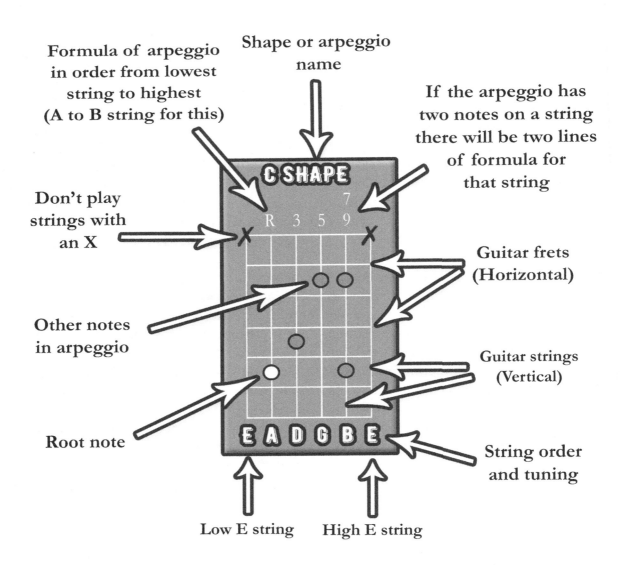

Formula of arpeggio in order from lowest string to highest (A to B string for this)

Shape or arpeggio name

If the arpeggio has two notes on a string there will be two lines of formula for that string

Don't play strings with an X

Other notes in arpeggio

Root note

Guitar frets (Horizontal)

Guitar strings (Vertical)

String order and tuning

Low E string   High E string

As mentioned in the introduction, I highly recommend you learn all the notes on the fretboard so you can move these arpeggio shapes around; there is a full fretboard diagram later in this book that can help you. At first, I suggest learning any notes without sharps or flats on the low E, A and D strings, then you can fill in the gaps later.

What is an Arpeggio?

An arpeggio is a broken chord where the notes are played individually, and not all together like if you were strumming a chord. To give you an example, in the first bar of the notation below you will see an E major chord (C Shape) and in the second bar it's arpeggio which has been broken apart and picked separately.

These can be extremely useful for improvising and navigating your way around the guitar fretboard. As mentioned in the introduction, they are closely related to the sweep picking technique but you do not need to be a great sweep picker to utilise arpeggio shapes and I will show you many other fun alternatives in this book.

By using arpeggios in your improvisation, you can target chord tones for each change in the progression and happily know each note will sound great. You may have noticed in the notation above that there are some symbols above the tablature and some numbers. The symbols show whether you should use an upstroke or downstroke with you picking hand and the numbers are suggestions for finger positions for the fretting hand of the arpeggios:

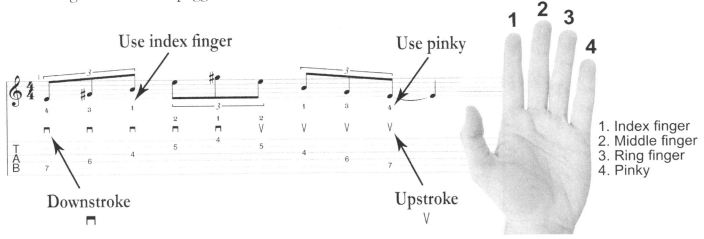

1. Index finger
2. Middle finger
3. Ring finger
4. Pinky

I recommend when first learning the arpeggio shapes in this book you practice them from the root note to get used to where they can be played in different keys.

Guitar Intervals in The Key Of D

Here are all the intervals on the fretboard in the key of D (most of the exercises in this book are in the key of D). You can use this to visualize how the arpeggio shapes are formed with the formulas. There is a total of 12 notes on the fretboard that just repeat in octaves over the different strings (based on standard tuning).

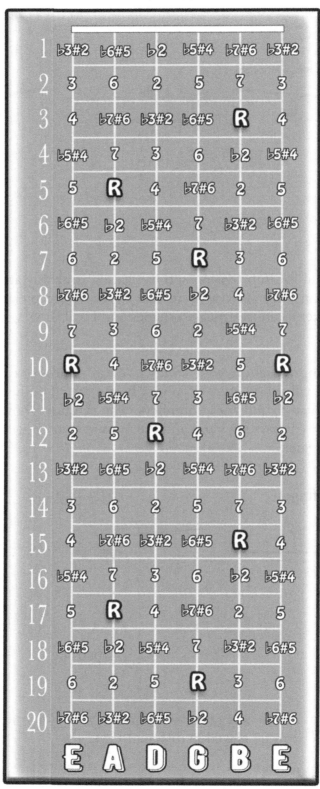

Notes On the Fretboard

Here are all the notes on the fretboard with standard tuning. It is worth spending some time to learn these as it will help you move the arpeggio shapes given in this book to any key you desire. Notice that the high and low E strings have exactly the same note order but two octaves apart, so there are only another four strings to learn after that!

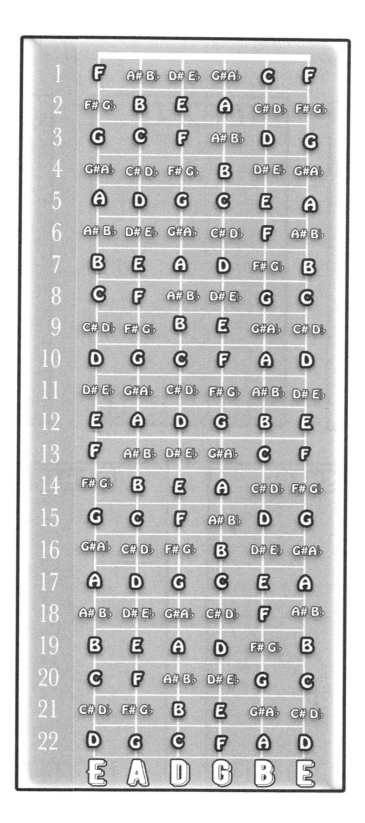

Major Triad Arpeggios
Formula (R, 3, 5)

Major triad arpeggios are formed with the root, major third and perfect fifth. Using the CAGED system (see back of book), below are five movable shapes that allow you to play the major arpeggios all over the fretboard. Don't worry if you don't understand how the CAGED system works, it is more important that you understand that by using the root note you can move these shapes to any key you want on the fretboard. As with all arpeggios the formula root, third and fifth just repeat to form these shapes. These arpeggios sound great over major, major seventh, major ninth, major eleventh and major thirteenth chords.

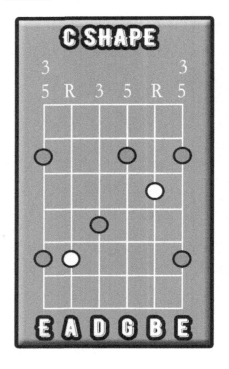
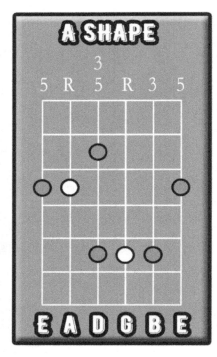
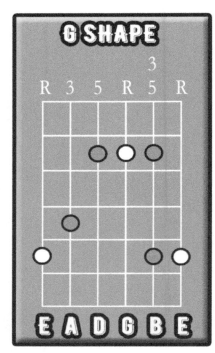

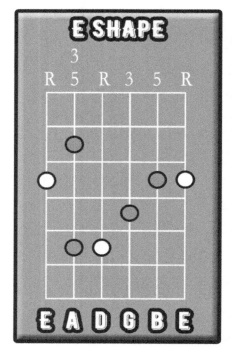
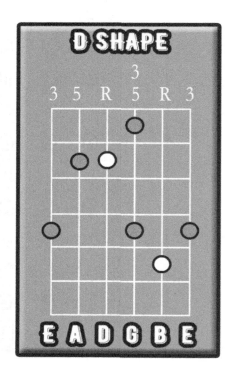

Practising Major Triad Arpeggios

Below are some practice ideas to help learn each of the major arpeggio CAGED shapes in the key of D. I recommend practising from the root note like the exercises below as this will help you move the shapes around more smoothly when changing key. Make sure you pay close attention to the picking strokes, hammer-ons and pull-offs, as well as the left-hand finger recommendations as this will help organise your fingers without moving position.

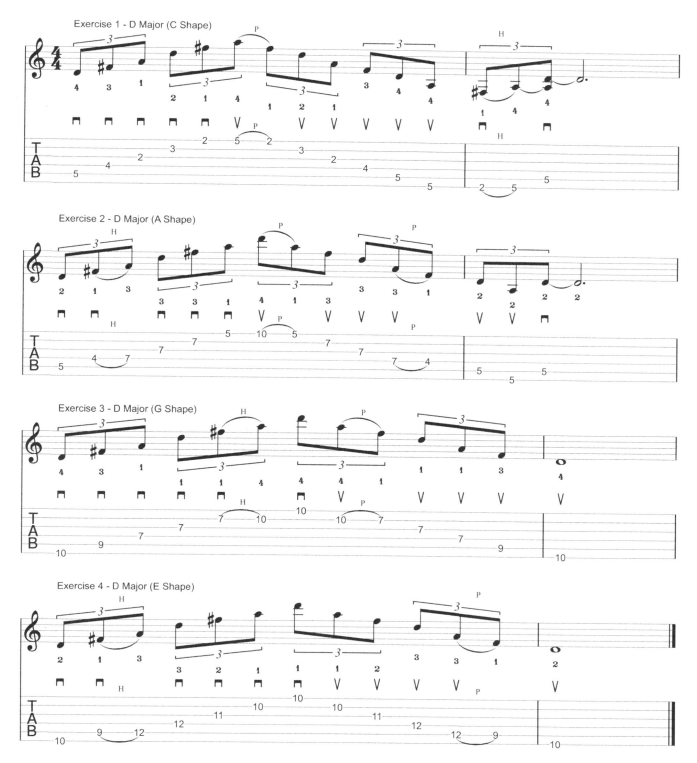

Exercise 5 - D Major (D Shape)

Another great way to practice these shapes is to play in every key using the circle of fifths (see back of book).

Below are two alternative shapes that are very useful for the CAGED A and D major arpeggio shapes that you can experiment with as well:

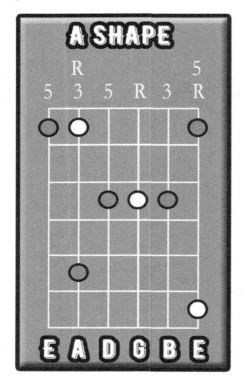

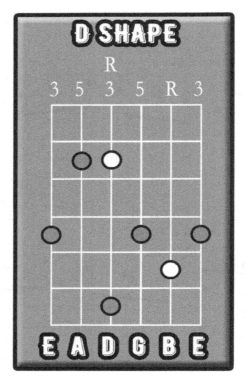

If you are new to arpeggios you may find it tricky to play shapes that use your pinky. Don't panic, just take it slow and eventually you will not even think about it. I have been playing guitar for years and I wish I had made more effort earlier on with the trickier hand positions as logically if you tackle every possible finger position early on you will not have to think about it later on in your playing.

Another tricky part of playing some arpeggio shapes is barring notes on the same fret known as 'finger rolling'. Visit **www.karlgolden.org/ultimateguitarseries** for some tips on how to nail this technique. Later on in this book we look at other methods to avoid barring with string skipping and tapped arpeggios!

Minor Triad Arpeggios
Formula (R, ♭3, 5)

Minor arpeggios are formed with the root, minor third and perfect fifth. Using the CAGED system, below are five movable shapes that allow you to play minor arpeggios all over the fretboard. These arpeggios sound great over minor, minor seventh, minor eleventh and minor thirteenth chords.

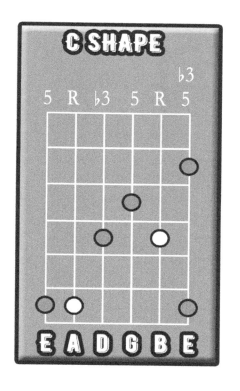

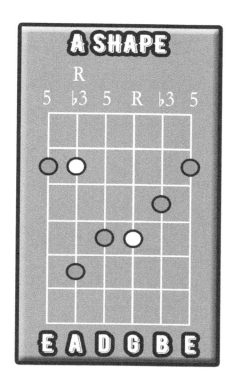

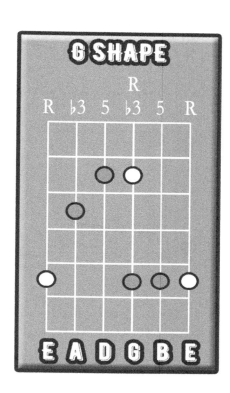

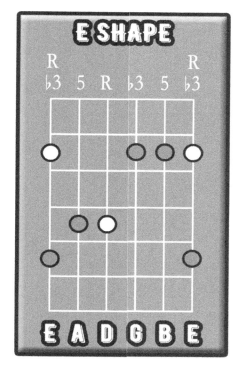

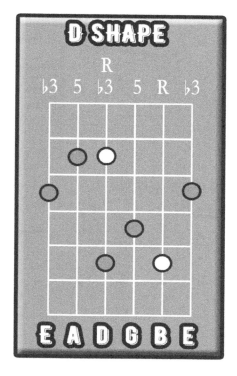

Practising Minor Triad Arpeggios

Below are some practice ideas to help learn each of the minor arpeggio CAGED shapes in the key of D. I recommend practising from the root note like the exercises below as this will help you move the shapes around more smoothly when changing key. Make sure you pay close attention to the picking strokes, hammer-ons and pull-offs, as well as the left-hand finger recommendations as this will help organise your fingers without moving position.

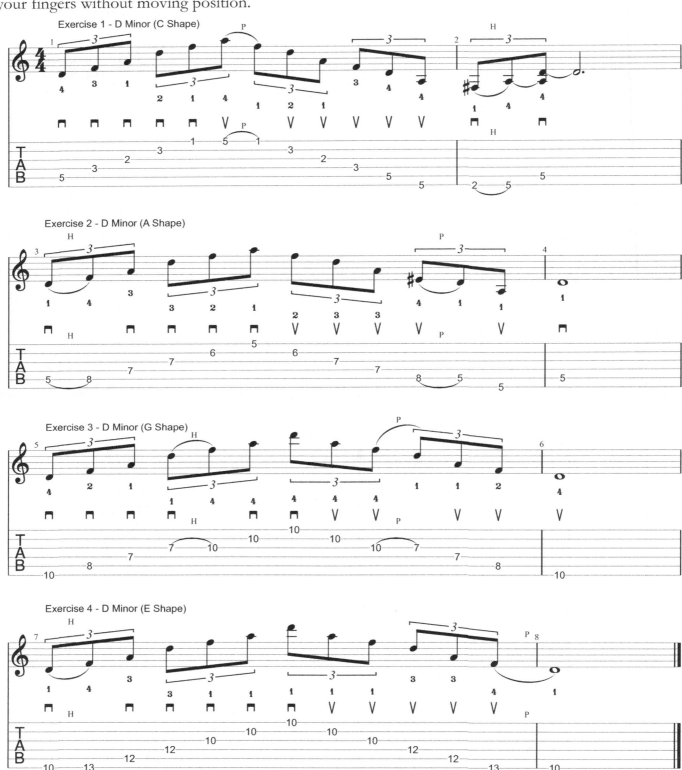

Exercise 5 - D Minor (D Shape)

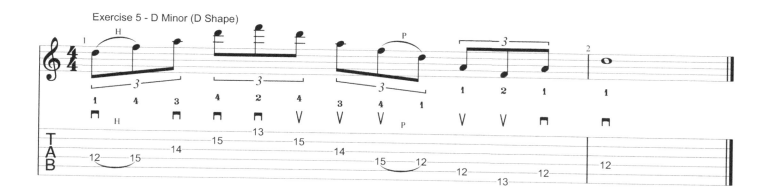

Diminished Triad Arpeggios

Formula (R, ♭3, ♭5)

Diminished triad arpeggios are formed with the root, minor third and diminished fifth. Using the CAGED system, below are five movable shapes that allow you to play diminished arpeggios all over the fretboard. These arpeggios sound great over diminished, half-diminished and fully-diminished chords.

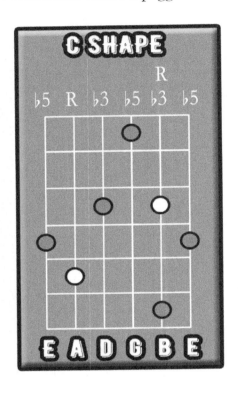

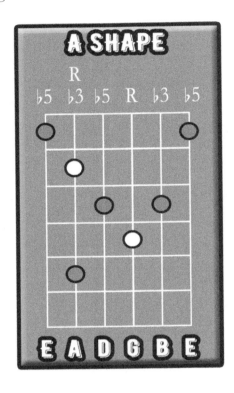

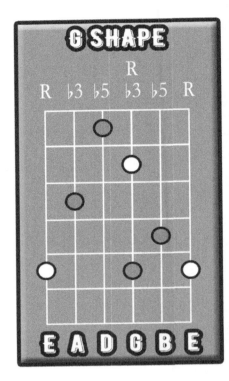

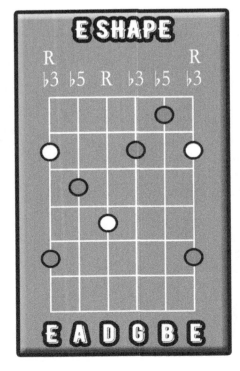

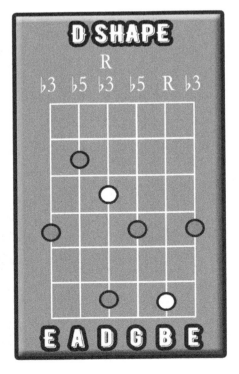

Practising Diminished Triad Arpeggios

Below are some practice ideas to help learn each of the diminished arpeggio CAGED shapes in the key of D. I recommend practising from the root note like the exercises below, as this will help you move the shapes around more smoothly when changing key. Make sure you pay close attention to the picking strokes, hammer-ons and pull-offs, as well as the left-hand finger recommendations as this will help organise your fingers without moving position.

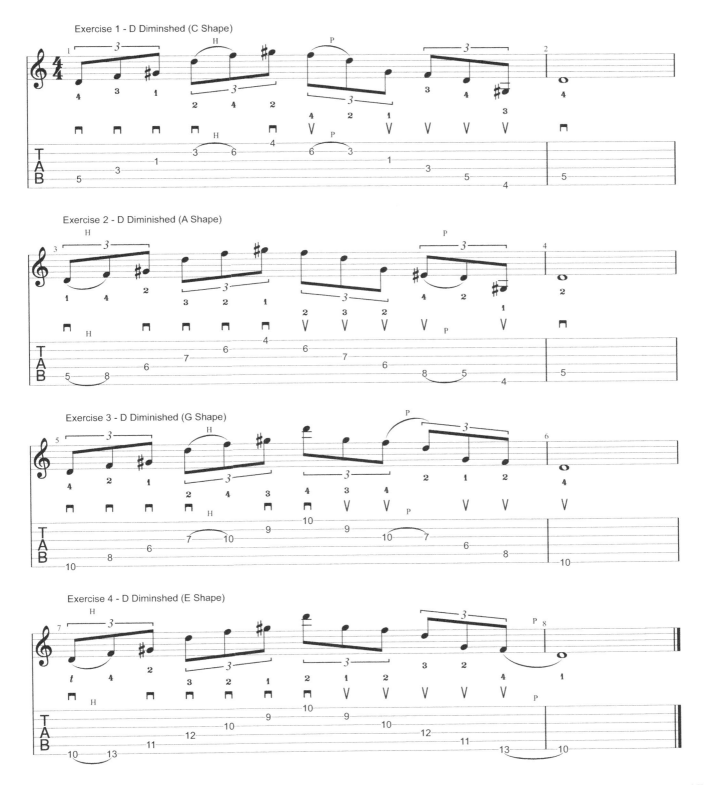

Exercise 5 - D Diminished (D Shape)

You will notice that some of these shapes are much easier to play than others. It is worth learning all shapes, but I recommend spending more time nailing shapes that feel comfortable at first to you then move onto the more complicated ones.

Augmented Triad Arpeggios
Formula (R, 3, #5)

Augmented arpeggios are formed with the root, minor third and augmented fifth. Using the CAGED system, below are five movable shapes that allow you to play augmented arpeggios all over the fretboard. These arpeggios sound great over major augmented chords.

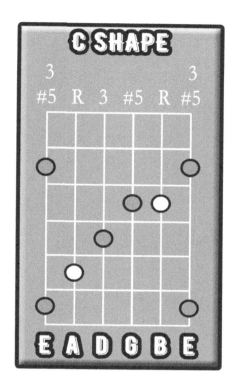

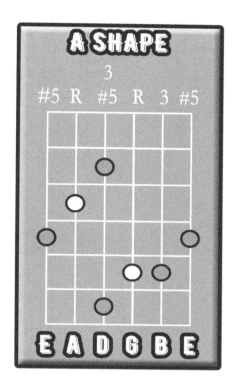

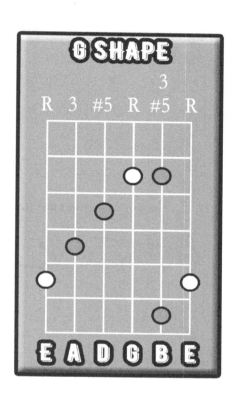

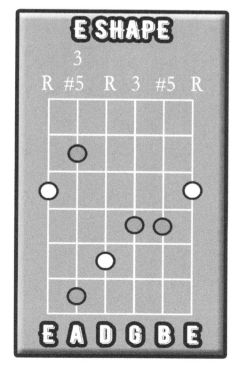

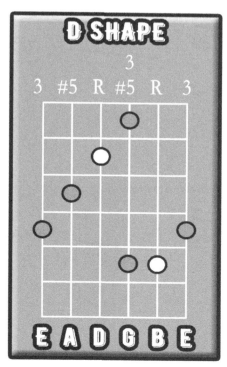

Practising Augmented Triad Arpeggios

Below are some practice ideas to help learn each of the augmented arpeggio CAGED shapes in the key of D. I recommend practising from the root note like the exercises below as this will help you move the shapes around more smoothly when changing key. Make sure you pay close attention to the picking strokes, hammer-ons and pull-offs, as well as the left-hand finger recommendations as this will help organise your fingers without moving position.

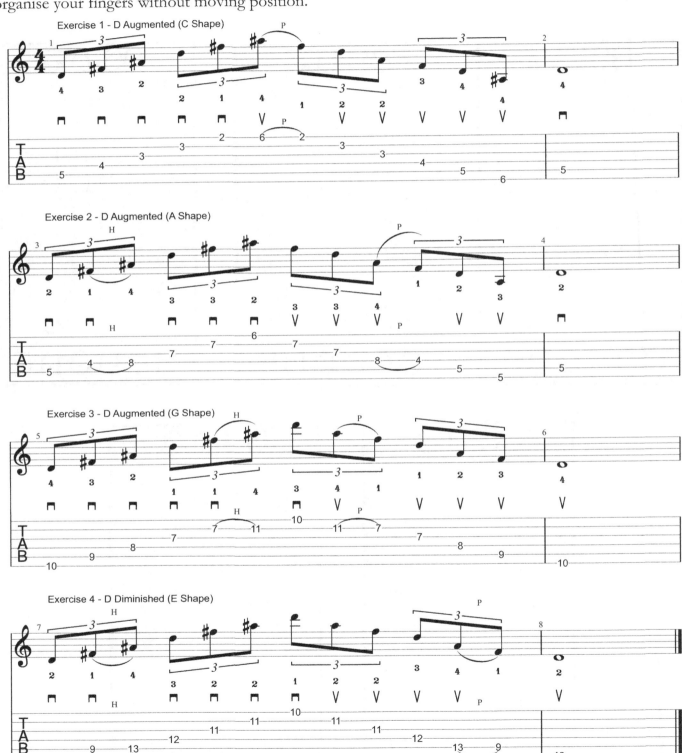

With exercise 1 and the C shape you cannot physically arrange the notes on the low E string to stay in line with the pattern. This is a good example of not needing to fully learn all the shapes as you would not realistically use this in your improvisation. Throughout this book you may find shapes that you connect with and others you don't, and that is fine. This book offers you a full range of shapes across the neck but in reality you may only use two or three of the shapes from the CAGED system, but it is still very important to practice shapes that are out of your comfort zone to train your fingers to go into positions they would not rather be. You will find in the future from practising every possible shape that it will really help with your other playing techniques.

Major Sixth Arpeggios
Formula (R, 3, 5, 6)

Major sixth arpeggios are formed with the root, major third, perfect fifth and major sixth. Using the CAGED system, below are five movable shapes that allow you to play major sixth arpeggios all over the fretboard. These arpeggios sound great over major sixth and other major chords.

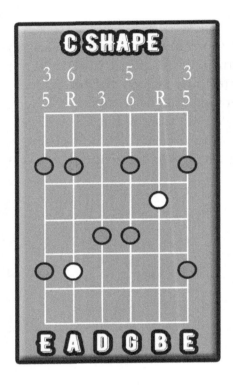

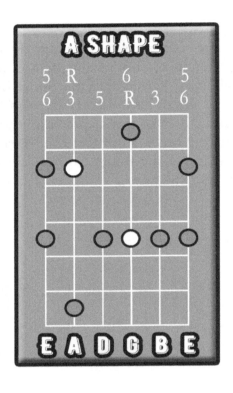

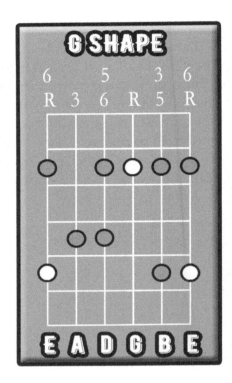

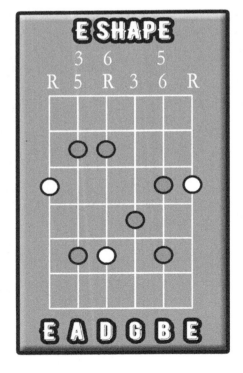

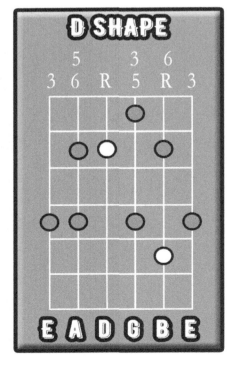

22

Practising Major Sixth Arpeggios

Below are some practice ideas to help learn each of the major six arpeggio CAGED shapes in the key of D. I recommend practising from the root note like the exercises below as this will help you move the shapes around more smoothly when changing key. Make sure you pay close attention to the picking strokes, hammer-ons and pull-offs, as well as the left-hand finger recommendations as this will help organise your fingers without moving position.

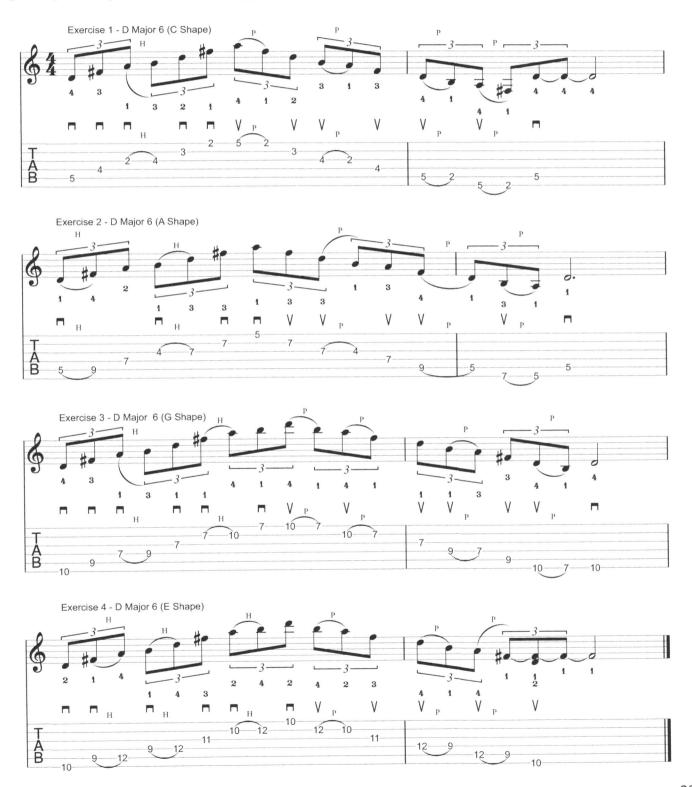

5. Exercise 5 - D Major 6 (D Shape)

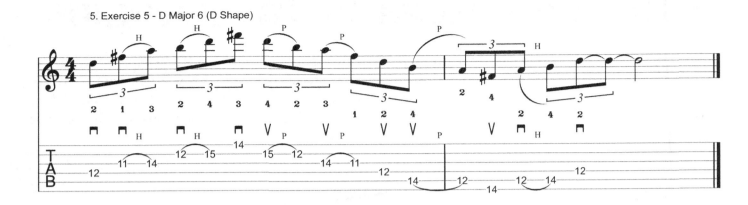

Minor Sixth Arpeggios
Formula (R, ♭3, 5, 6)

Minor sixth arpeggios are formed with the root, minor third, perfect fifth and major sixth. Using the CAGED system, below are five movable shapes that allow you to play minor sixth arpeggios all over the fretboard. These arpeggios sound great over minor sixth and other minor chords.

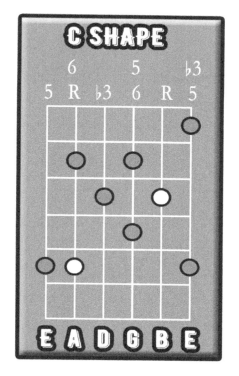

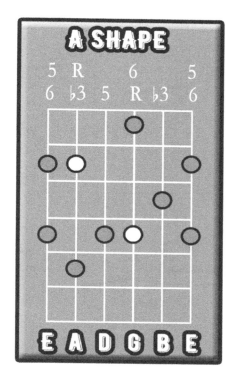

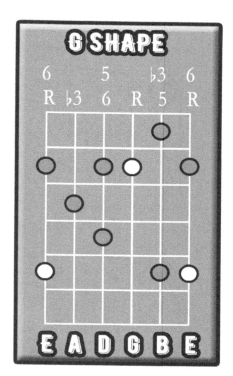

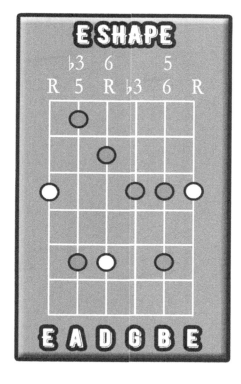

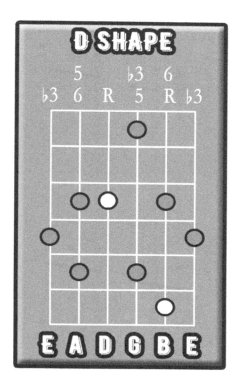

Practising Minor Sixth Arpeggios

Below are some practice ideas to help learn each of the minor six arpeggio CAGED shapes in the key of D. I recommend practising from the root note like the exercises below as this will help you move the shapes around more smoothly when changing key. Make sure you pay close attention to the picking strokes, hammer-ons and pull-offs, as well as the left-hand finger recommendations as this will help organise your fingers without moving position.

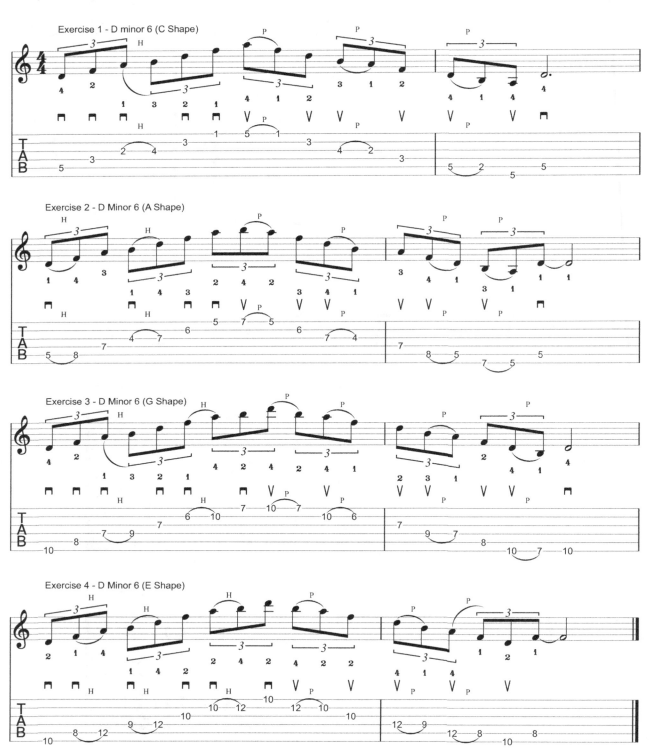

Exercise 5 - D Minor 6 (D Shape)

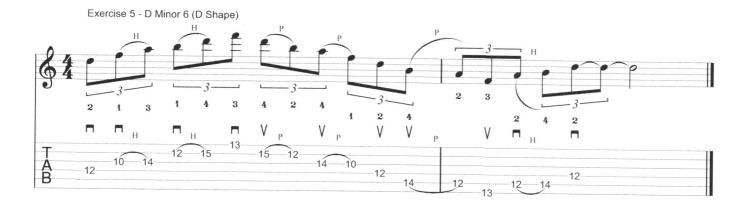

Major Seventh Arpeggios
Formula (R, 3, 5, 7)

Major seventh arpeggios are formed with the root, major third, perfect fifth and major seventh. Using the CAGED system, below are five movable shapes that allow you to play major seventh arpeggios all over the fretboard. These arpeggios sound great over major, major seventh, major ninth, major eleventh and major thirteenth chords.

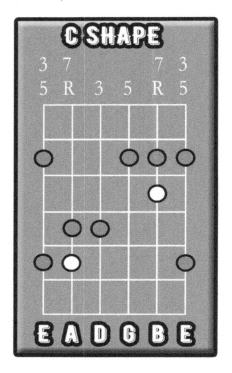

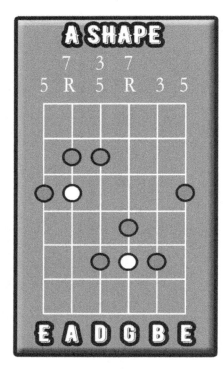

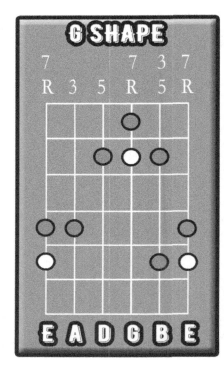

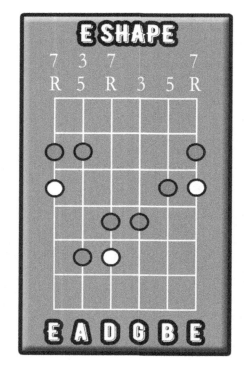

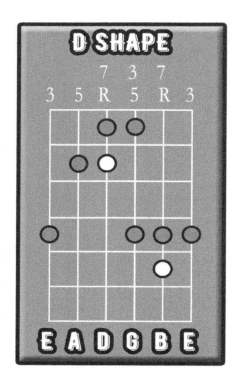

Practising Major Seventh Arpeggios

Below are some practice ideas to help learn each of the major seventh arpeggio CAGED shapes in the key of D. I recommend practising from the root note like the exercises below as this will help you move the shapes around more smoothly when changing key. Make sure you pay close attention to the picking strokes, hammer-ons and pull-offs, as well as the left-hand finger recommendations as this will help organise your fingers without moving position.

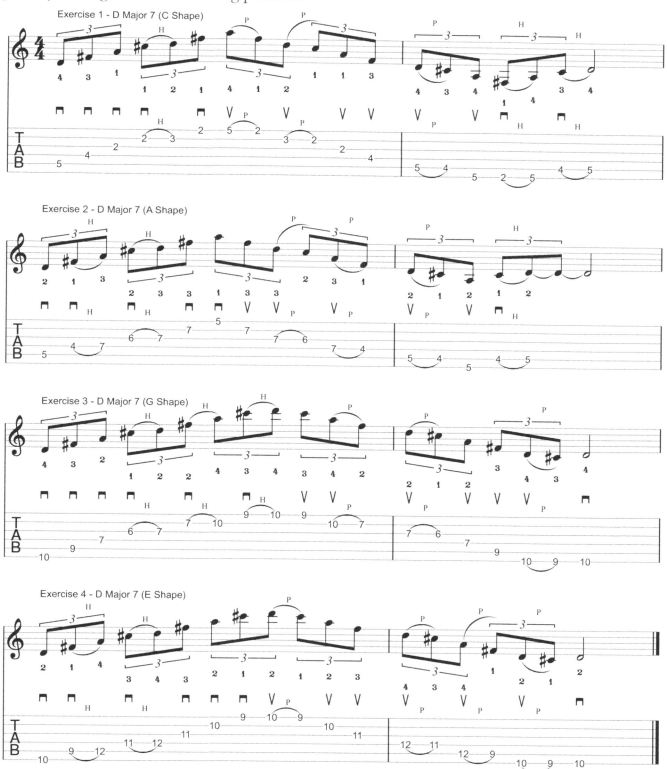

Exercise 5 - D Major 7 (D Shape)

Minor Seventh Arpeggios
Formula (R, ♭3, 5, ♭7)

Minor seventh arpeggios are formed with the root, minor third, perfect fifth and minor seventh. Using the CAGED system, below are five movable shapes that allow you to play minor seventh arpeggios all over the fretboard. These arpeggios sound great over minor, minor seventh, minor ninth, minor eleventh and minor thirteenth chords.

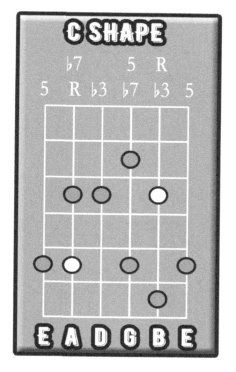

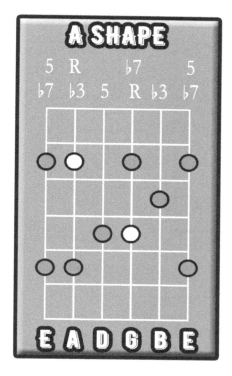

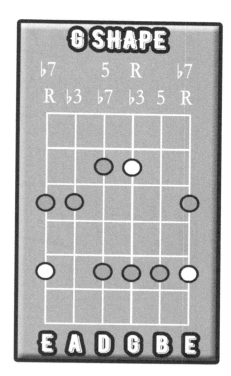

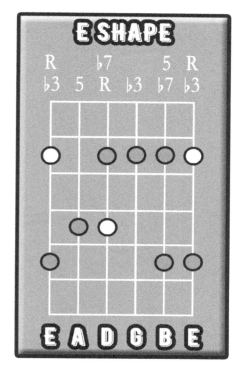

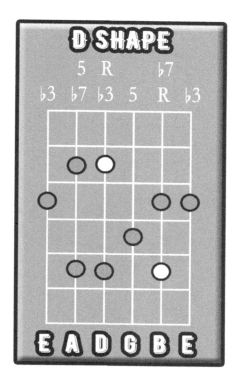

Practising Minor Seventh Arpeggios

Below are some practice ideas to help learn each of the minor seventh arpeggio CAGED shapes in the key of D. I recommend practising from the root note like the exercises below as this will help you move the shapes around more smoothly when changing key. Make sure you pay close attention to the picking strokes, hammer-ons and pull-offs, as well as the left-hand finger recommendations as this will help organise your fingers without moving position.

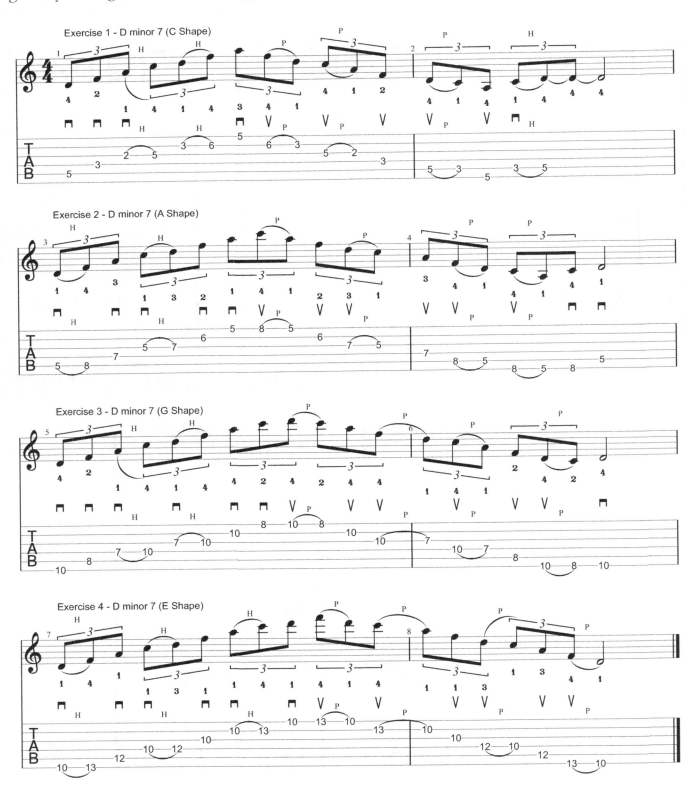

Exercise 5 - D minor 7 (D Shape)

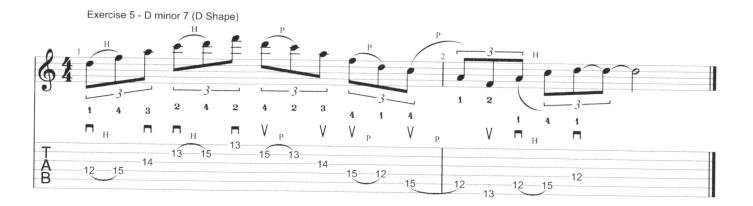

Dominant Seventh Arpeggios

Formula (R, 3, 5, ♭7)

Dominant seventh arpeggios are formed with the root, major third, perfect fifth and minor seventh. Using the CAGED system, below are five movable shapes that allow you to play dominant seventh arpeggios all over the fretboard. These arpeggios sound great over dominant seventh, dominant ninth, dominant eleventh and dominant thirteenth chords.

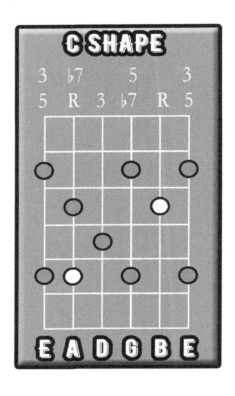

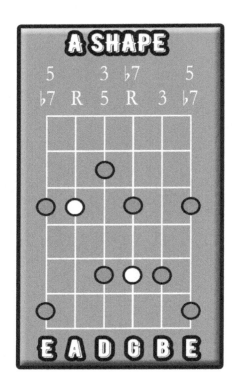

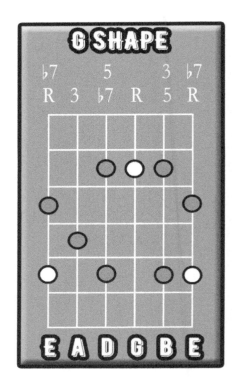

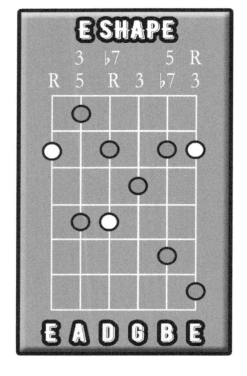

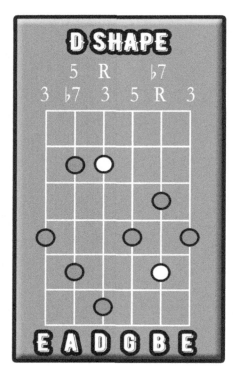

Practising Dominant Seventh Arpeggios

Below are some practice ideas to help learn each of the dominant seventh arpeggio CAGED shapes in the key of D. I recommend practising from the root note like the exercises below as this will help you move the shapes around more smoothly when changing key. Make sure you pay close attention to the picking strokes, hammer-ons and pull-offs, as well as the left-hand finger recommendations as this will help organise your fingers without moving position.

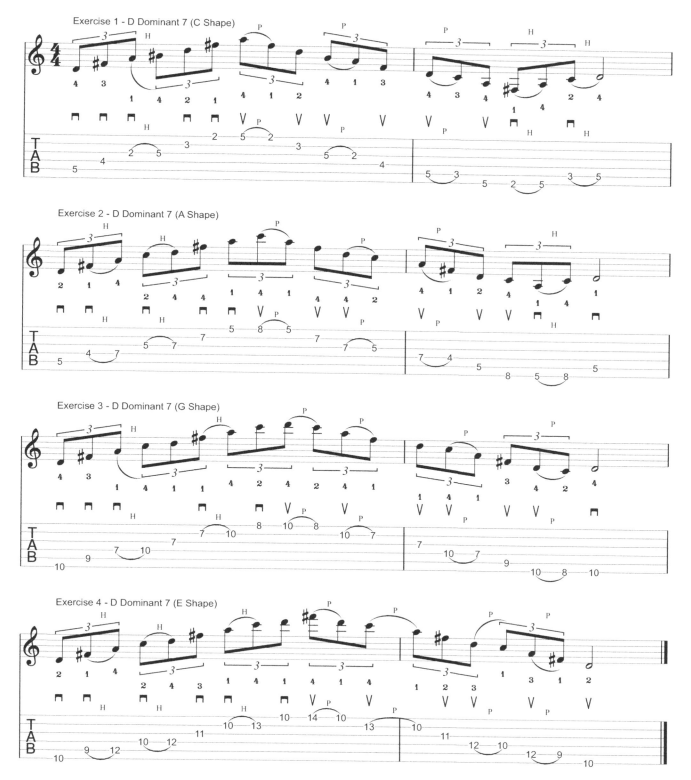

Exercise 5 - D Dominant 7 (D Shape)

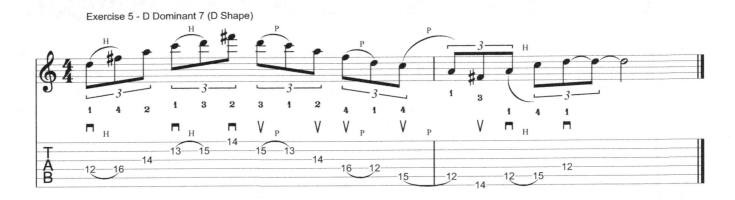

Half-Diminished Arpeggios
Formula (R, ♭3, ♭5, ♭7)

Half-diminished arpeggios, also known as minor seventh flat five arpeggios, are formed with the root, minor third, diminished fifth and minor seventh. Using the CAGED system, below are five movable shapes that allow you to play half-diminished seventh arpeggios all over the fretboard. These arpeggios sound great over half-diminished chords.

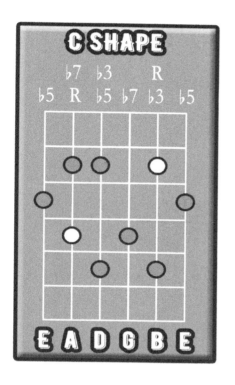

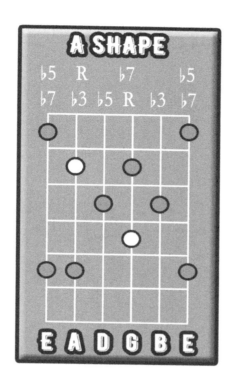

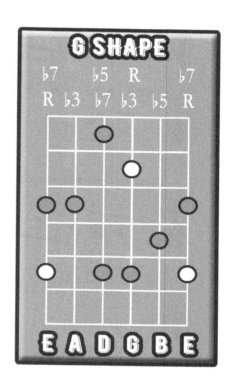

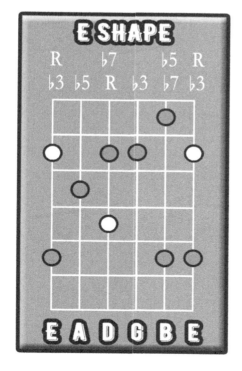

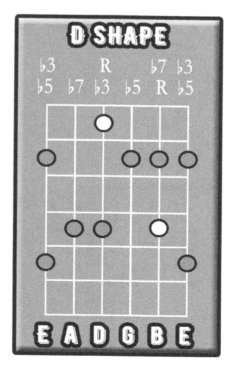

Practising Half-Diminished Seventh Arpeggios

Below are some practice ideas to help learn each of the half-diminished seventh arpeggio CAGED shapes in the key of D. I recommend practising from the root note like the exercises below as this will help you move the shapes around more smoothly when changing key. Make sure you pay close attention to the picking strokes, hammer-ons and pull-offs, as well as the left-hand finger recommendations as this will help organise your fingers without moving position.

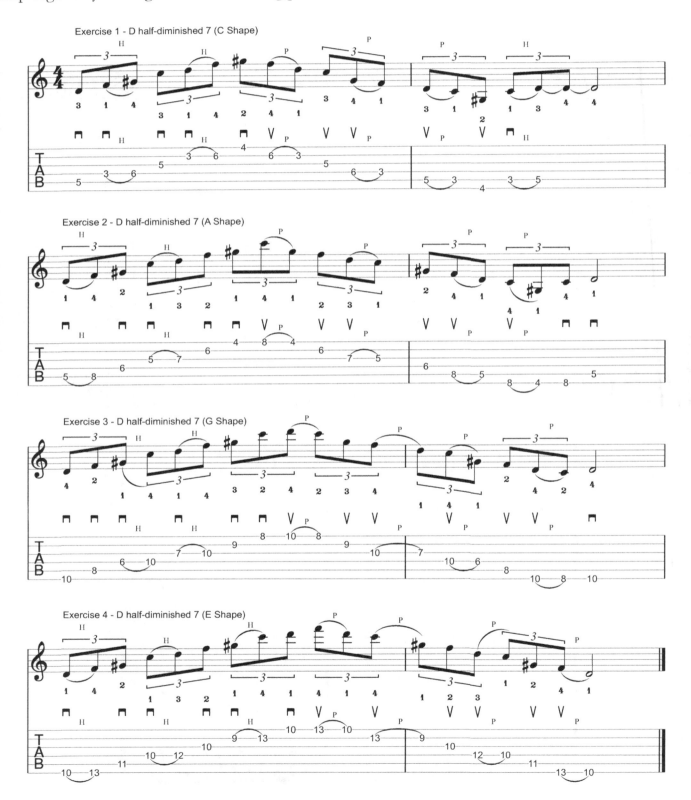

Exercise 5 - D half-diminished 7 (D Shape)

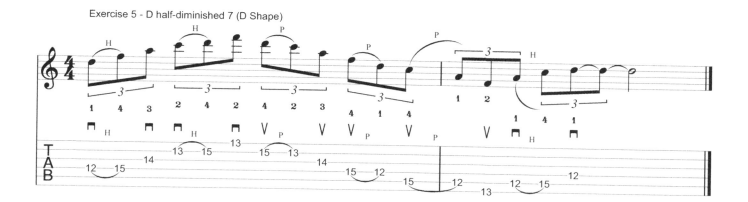

Fully-Diminished Seventh Arpeggios

Formula (R, ♭3, ♭5, ♭♭7)

Fully-diminished seventh arpeggios are formed with the root, minor third, diminished fifth and diminished seventh. A diminished seventh note is equivalent to a major sixth - to avoid any confusion! Using the CAGED system, below are five movable shapes that allow you to play the fully-diminished seventh arpeggios all over the fretboard. These arpeggios sound great over fully-diminished chords.

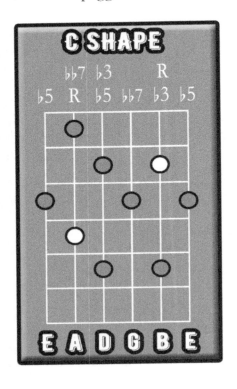

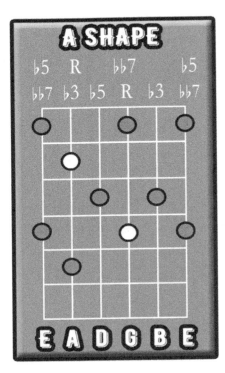

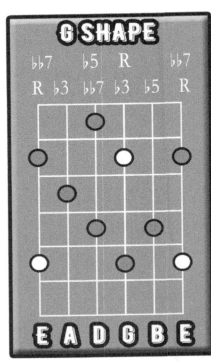

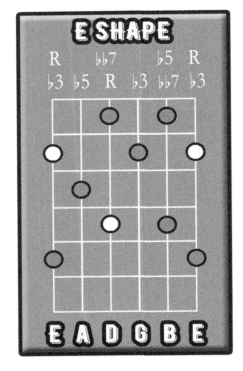

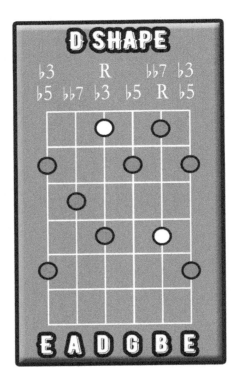

Practising Fully-Diminished Seventh Arpeggios

Below are some practice ideas to help learn each of the fully-diminished seventh arpeggio CAGED shapes in the key of D. I recommend practising from the root note like the exercises below as this will help you move the shapes around more smoothly when changing key. Make sure you pay close attention to the picking strokes, hammer-ons and pull-offs, as well as the left-hand finger recommendations as this will help organise your fingers without moving position.

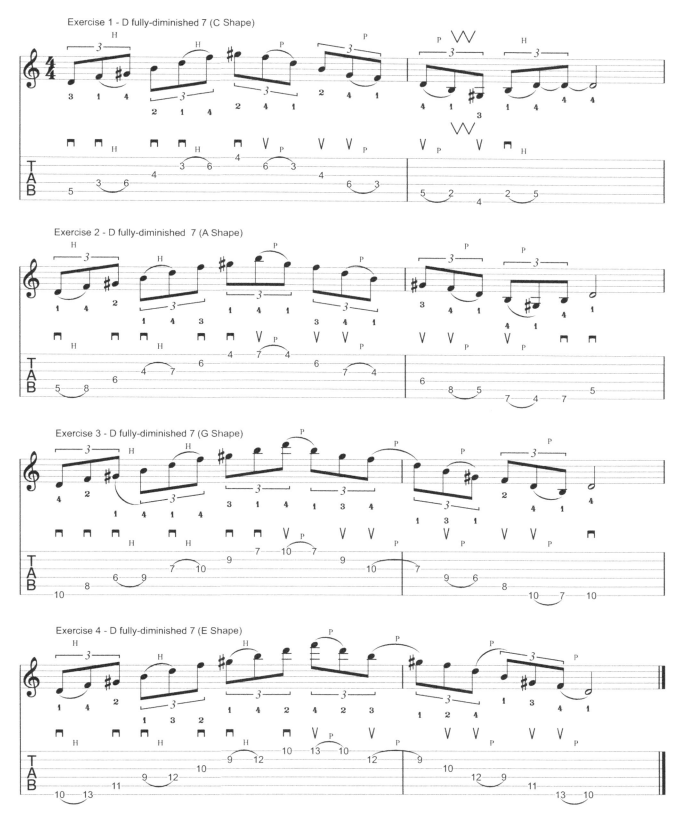

41

Exercise 5 - D fully-diminished 7 (D Shape)

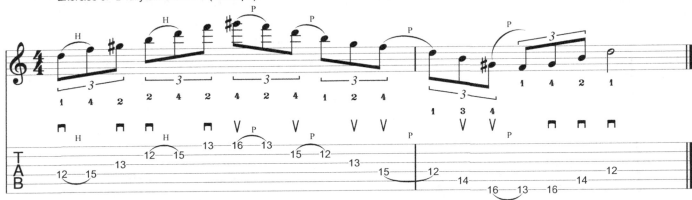

Minor Major Seventh Arpeggios
Formula (R, ♭3, 5, 7)

Minor major seventh arpeggios are formed with the root, minor third, perfect fifth and major seventh. The minor third gives the arpeggio the minor quality and the natural seventh gives it that major sound. Using the CAGED system, below are five movable shapes that allow you to play the minor major seventh arpeggio all over the fretboard. These arpeggios sound great over minor major seventh chords.

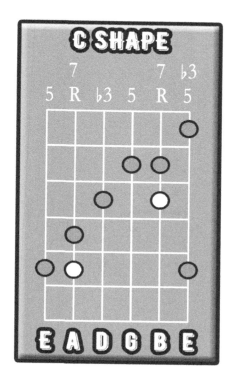

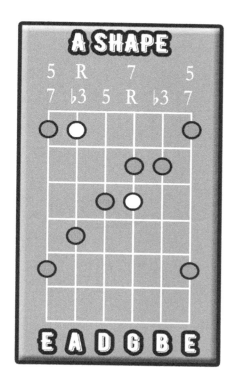

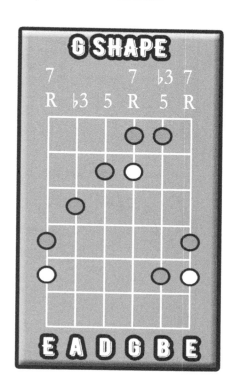

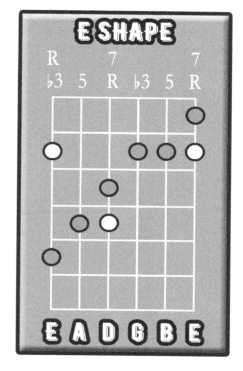

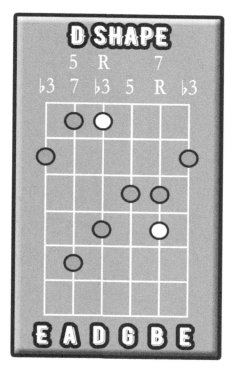

Practising Minor Major Seventh Arpeggios

Below are some practice ideas to help learn each of the minor major seventh arpeggio CAGED shapes in the key of D. I recommend practising from the root note like the exercises below as this will help you move the shapes around more smoothly when changing key. Make sure you pay close attention to the picking strokes, hammer-ons and pull-offs, as well as the left-hand finger recommendations as this will help organise your fingers without moving position.

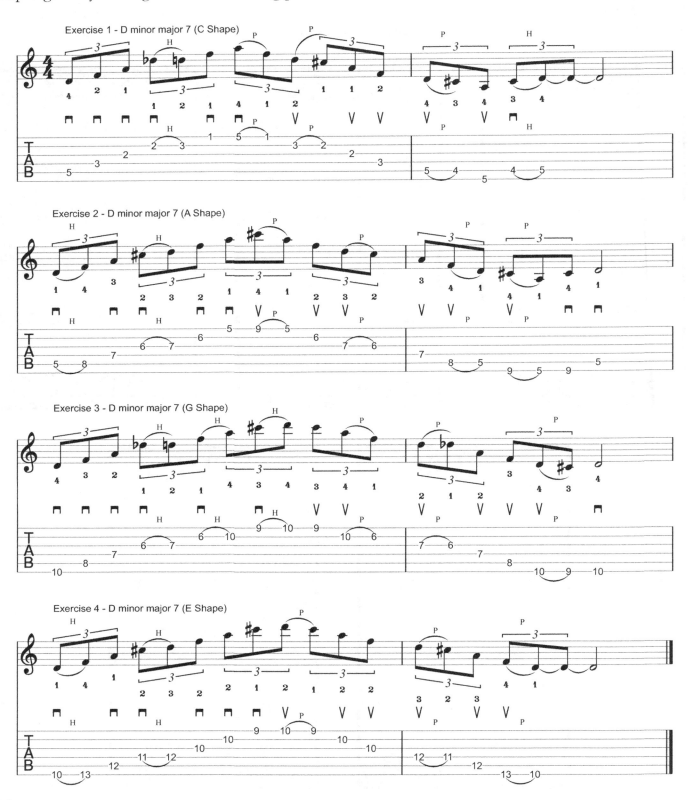

Exercise 5 - D minor major 7 (D Shape)

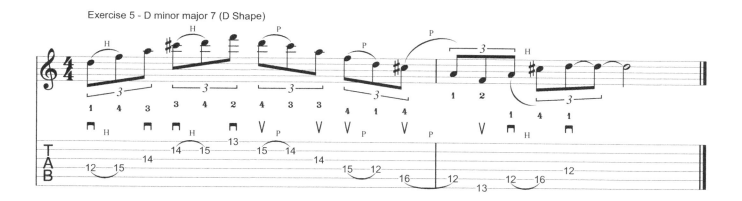

Major Seven Flat Five Arpeggios
Formula (R, 3, ♭5, 7)

Major seven flat five arpeggios are formed with the root, major third, diminished fifth and major seventh. Using the CAGED system, below are five movable shapes that allow you to play the major seven flat five arpeggio all over the fretboard. These arpeggios sound great over major seven flat five chords.

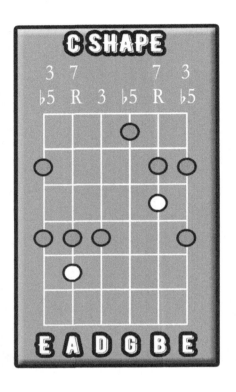

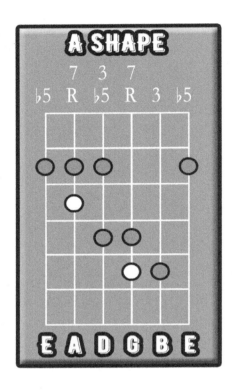

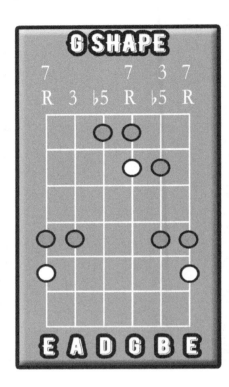

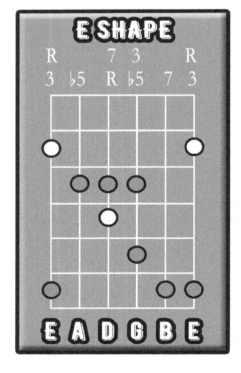

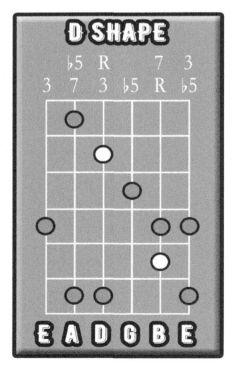

Practising Major Seven Flat Five Arpeggios

Below are some practice ideas to help learn each of the major seven flat five arpeggio CAGED shapes in the key of D. I recommend practising from the root note like the exercises below as this will help you move the shapes around more smoothly when changing key. Make sure you pay close attention to the picking strokes, hammer-ons and pull-offs, as well as the left-hand finger recommendations as this will help organise your fingers without moving position.

Exercise 5 - D Major 7 flat 5 (D Shape)

Major Seventh Sharp Five Arpeggios
Formula (R, 3, #5, 7)

Major seventh sharp five arpeggios are formed with the root, major third, augmented fifth and major seventh. Using the CAGED system, below are five movable shapes that allow you to play the major seventh sharp five arpeggios all over the fretboard. These arpeggios sound great over major seventh sharp five chords.

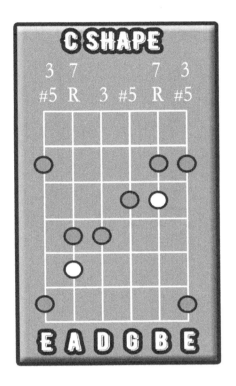

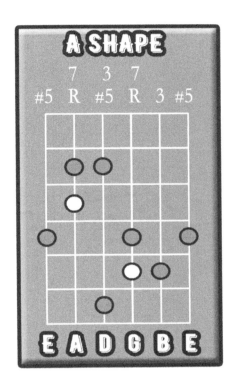

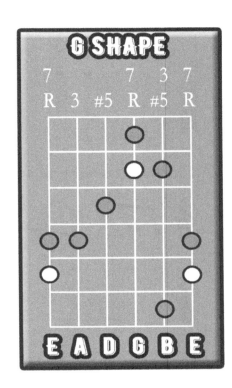

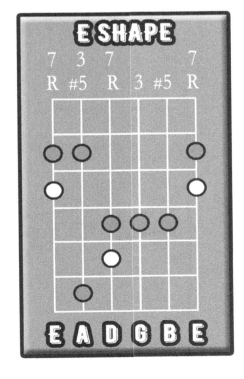

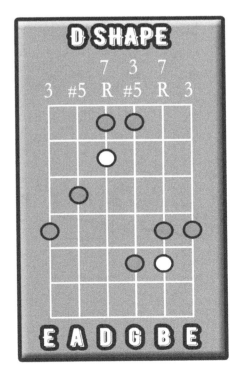

Practising Major Seven Sharp Five Arpeggios

Below are some practice ideas to help learn each of the major seventh sharp five arpeggio CAGED shapes in the key of D. I recommend practising from the root note like the exercises below as this will help you move the shapes around more smoothly when changing key. Make sure you pay close attention to the picking strokes, hammer-ons and pull-offs, as well as the left-hand finger recommendations as this will help organise your fingers without moving position.

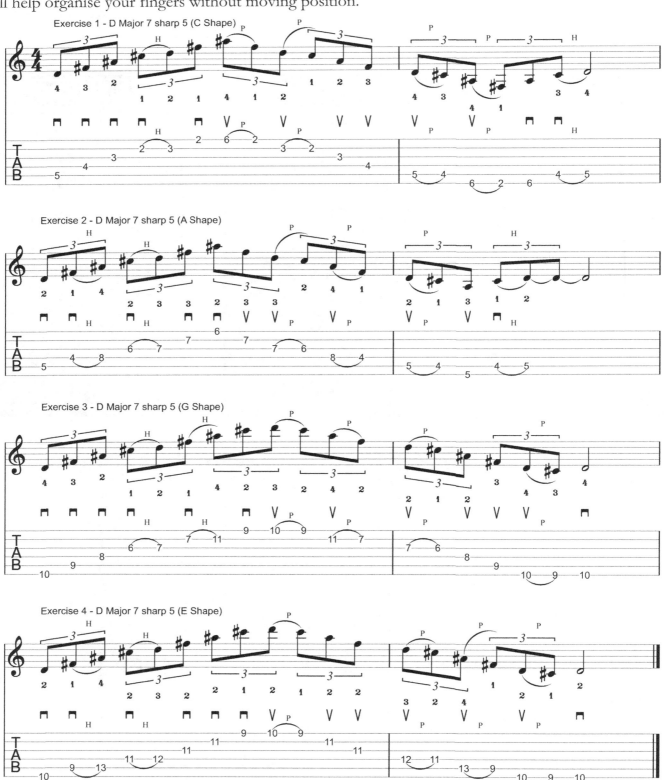

50

Exercise 5 - D Major 7 sharp 5 (D Shape)

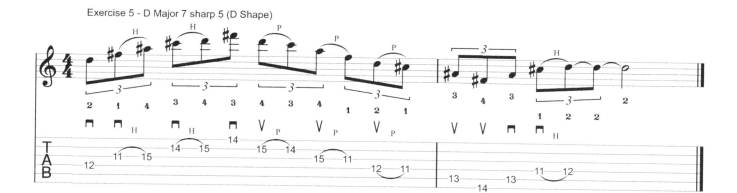

Major Ninth Arpeggios
Formula (R, 3, 5, 7, 9)

Major ninth arpeggios are formed with the root, major third, perfect fifth, major seventh and major ninth. The major ninth is actually a major second an octave up from the root. Using the CAGED system, below are five movable shapes that allow you to play the major ninth arpeggios all over the fretboard. These arpeggios sound great over major, major seventh, major ninth, major eleventh and major thirteenth chords.

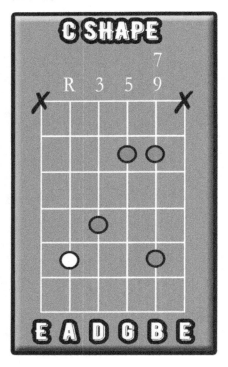

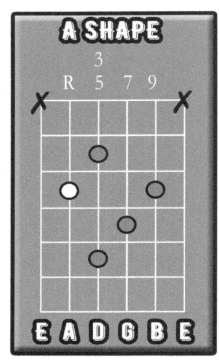

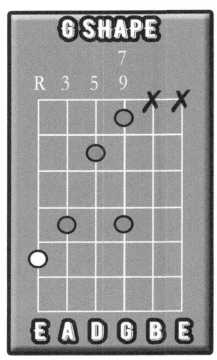

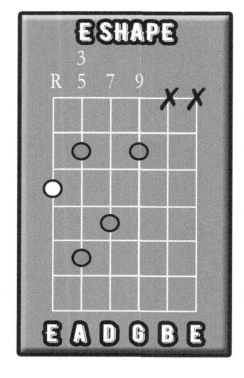

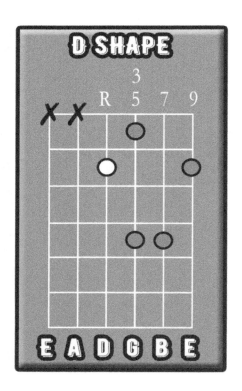

Practising Major Ninth Arpeggios

Below are some practice ideas to help learn each of the major ninth arpeggio CAGED shapes in the key of D. I recommend practising from the root note like the exercises below as this will help you move the shapes around more smoothly when changing key. Make sure you pay close attention to the picking strokes, hammer-ons and pull-offs, as well as the left-hand finger recommendations as this will help organise your fingers without moving position.

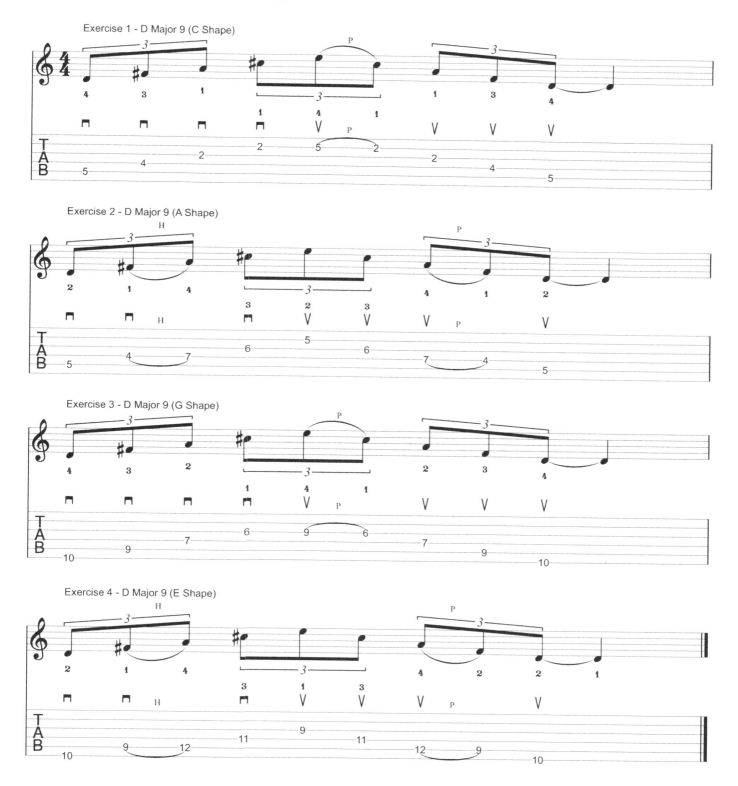

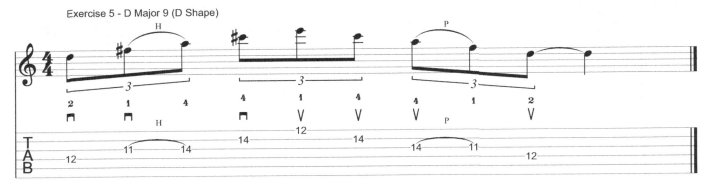

Exercise 5 - D Major 9 (D Shape)

Below are three alternative shapes that are very useful for the A, E and D major ninth arpeggio that you can experiment with as well:

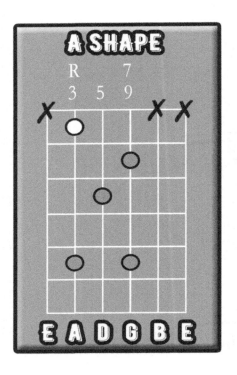

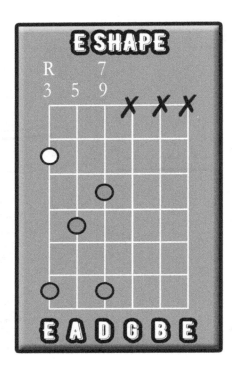

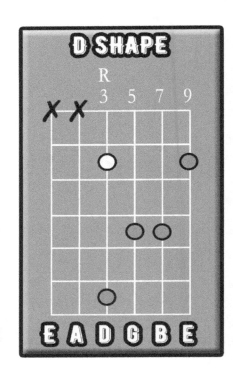

Minor Ninth Arpeggios
Formula (R, ♭3, 5, ♭7, 9)

Minor ninth arpeggios are formed with the root, minor third, perfect fifth, minor seventh and major ninth. The major ninth is actually a major second an octave up from the root. Using the CAGED system, below are five movable shapes that allow you to play the same minor ninth arpeggios all over the fretboard. These arpeggios sound great over minor, minor seventh, minor ninth, minor eleventh and minor thirteenth chords.

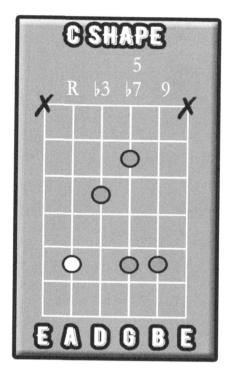

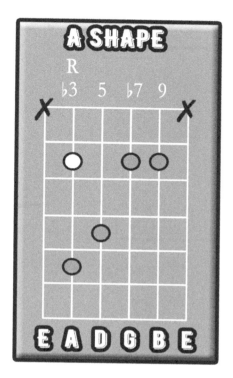

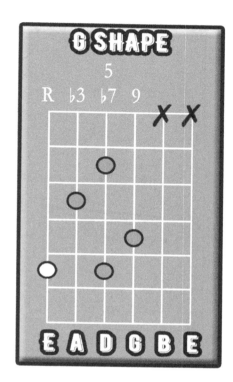

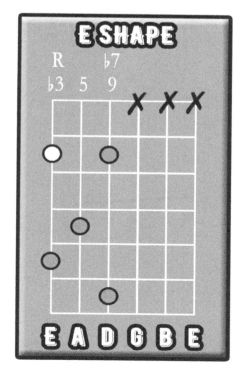

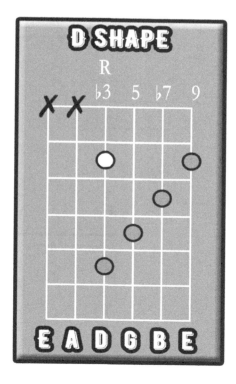

Practising Minor Ninth Arpeggios

Below are some practice ideas to help learn each of the minor ninth arpeggio CAGED shapes in the key of D. I recommend practising from the root note like the exercises below as this will help you move the shapes around more smoothly when changing key. Make sure you pay close attention to the picking strokes, hammer-ons and pull-offs, as well as the left-hand finger recommendations as this will help organise your fingers without moving position.

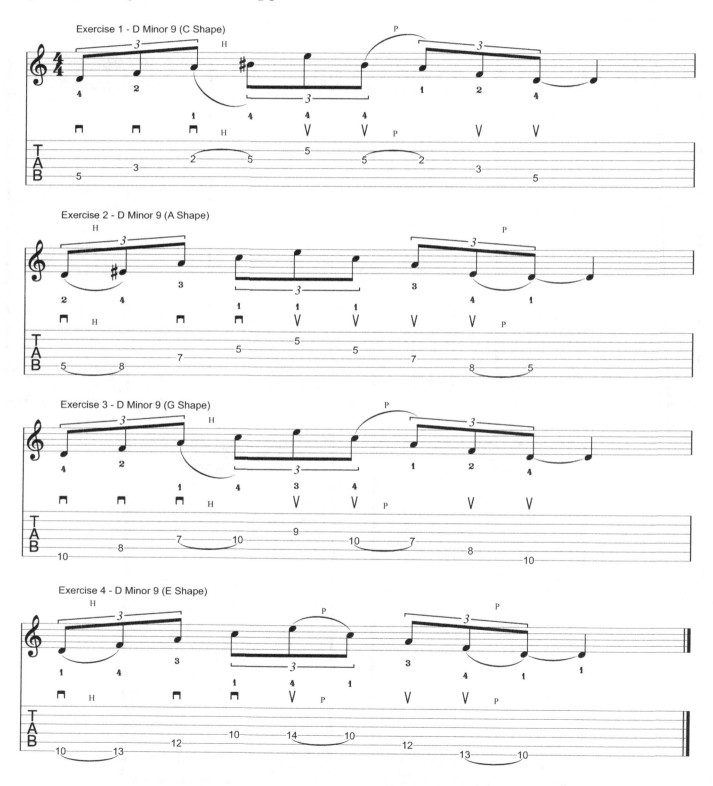

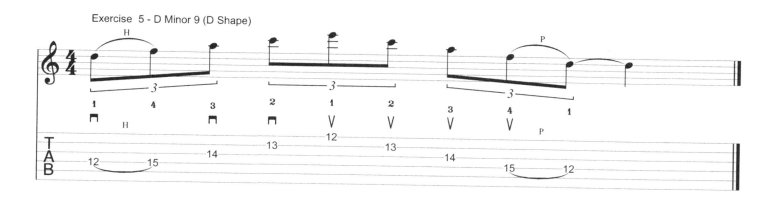

Exercise 5 - D Minor 9 (D Shape)

Dominant Ninth Arpeggios
Formula (R, 3, 5, ♭7, 9)

Dominant ninth arpeggios are formed with the root, major third, perfect fifth, minor seventh and major ninth. The major ninth is actually a major second an octave up from the root. Using the CAGED system, below are five movable shapes that allow you to play the dominant ninth arpeggios all over the fretboard. These arpeggios sound great over dominant seventh, dominant ninth, dominant eleventh and dominant thirteenth chords.

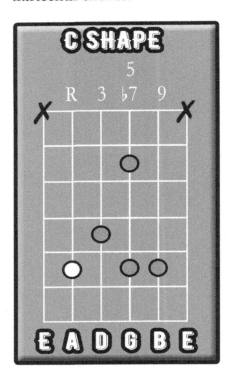
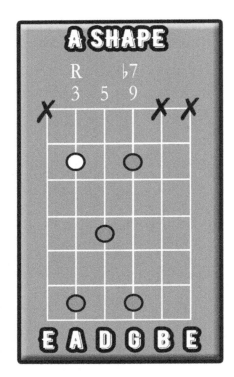
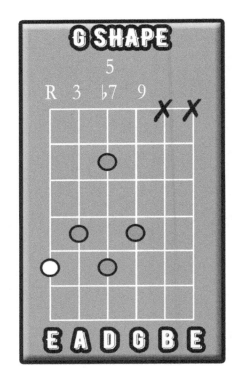

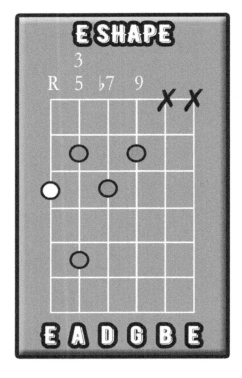
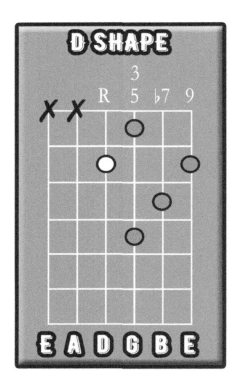

Practising Dominant Ninth Arpeggios

Below are some practice ideas to help learn each of the dominant ninth arpeggio CAGED shapes in the key of D. I recommend practising from the root note like the exercises below as this will help you move the shapes around more smoothly when changing key. Make sure you pay close attention to the picking strokes, hammer-ons and pull-offs, as well as the left-hand finger recommendations as this will help organise your fingers without moving position.

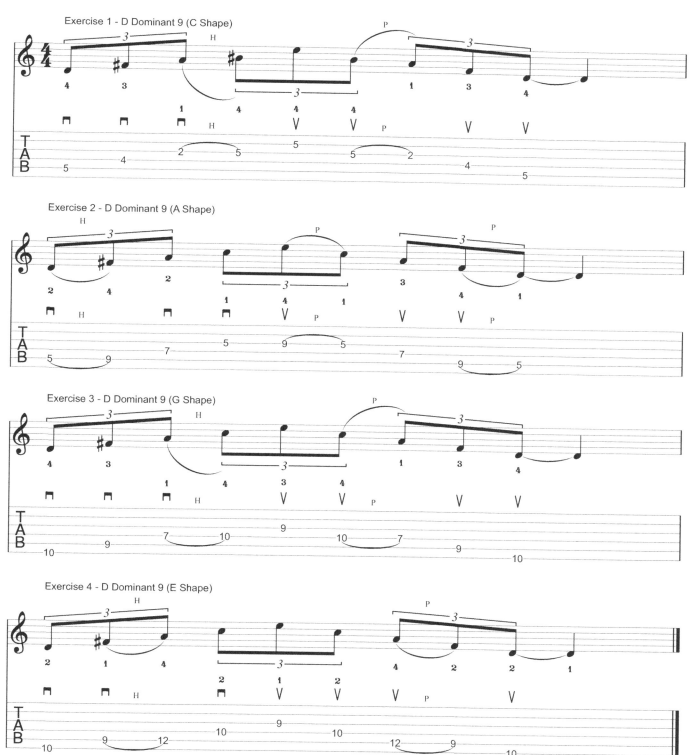

Exercise 5 - D Dominant 9 (D Shape)

Major Eleventh Arpeggios
Formula (R, 3, 5, 7, 9, 11)

Major eleventh arpeggios are formed with the root, major third, perfect fifth, major seventh, major ninth and major eleventh. The major eleventh is actually a perfect fourth an octave up from the root. Using the CAGED system, below are five movable shapes that allow you to play the major eleventh arpeggios all over the fretboard. These arpeggios sound great over major, major seventh, major ninth, major eleventh and major thirteenth chords.

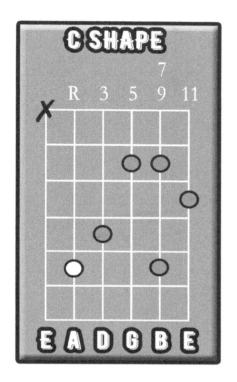

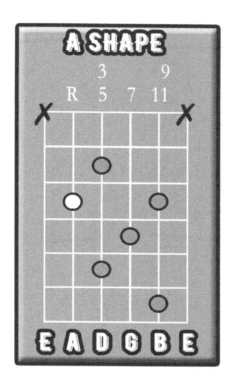

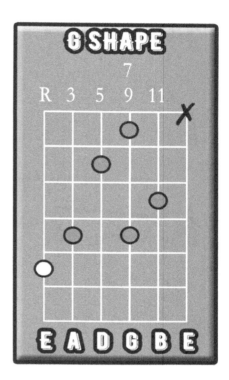

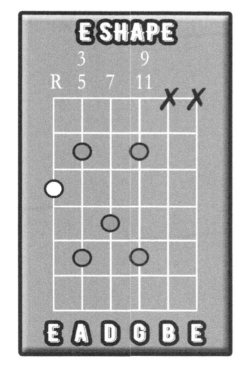

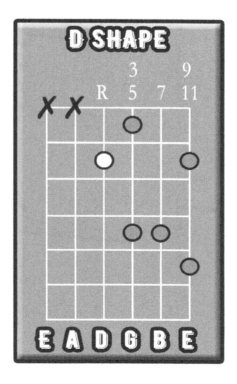

Practising Major Eleventh Arpeggios

Below are some practice ideas to help learn each of the major eleventh arpeggio CAGED shapes in the key of D. I recommend practising from the root note like the exercises below as this will help you move the shapes around more smoothly when changing key. Make sure you pay close attention to the picking strokes, hammer-ons and pull-offs, as well as the left-hand finger recommendations as this will help organise your fingers without moving position.

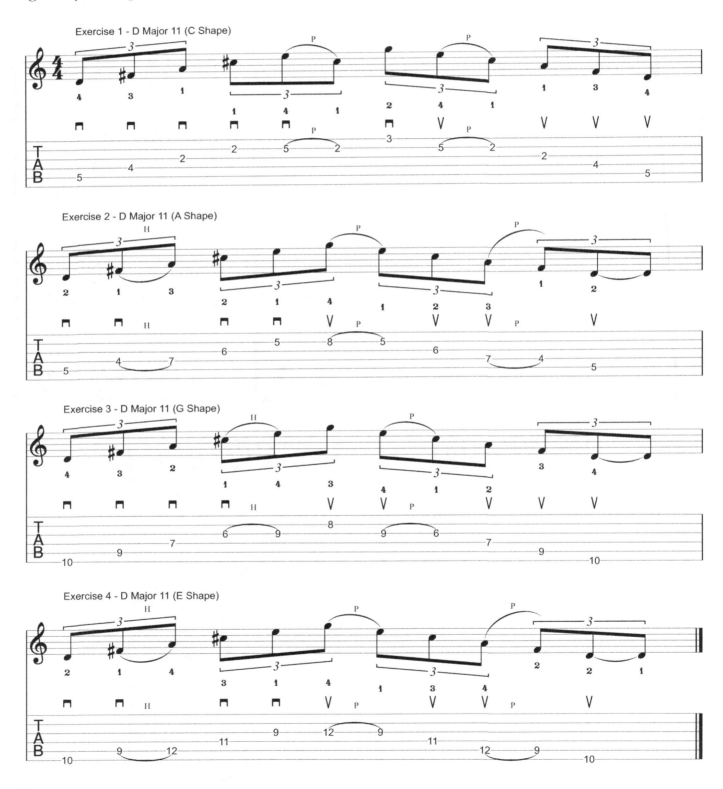

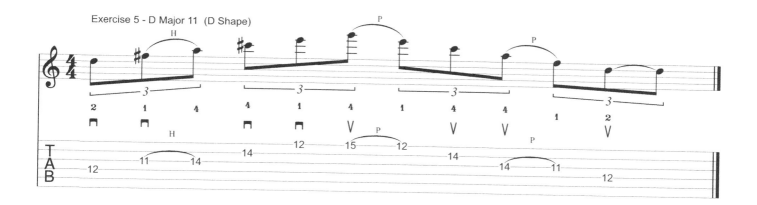

Exercise 5 - D Major 11 (D Shape)

Below are three alternative shapes that are very useful for the CAGED A, E and D major eleventh arpeggio that you can experiment with as well:

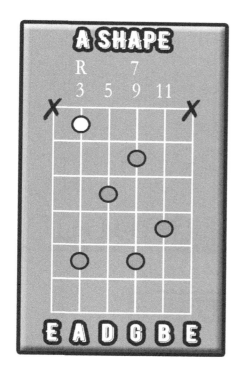

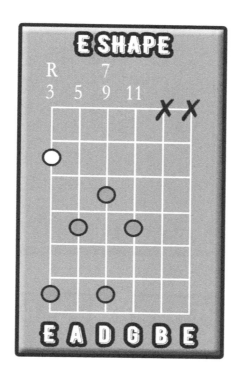

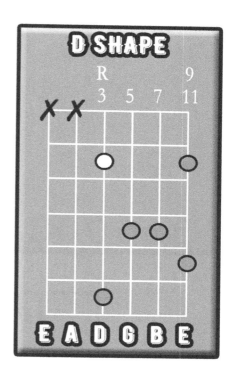

Minor Eleventh Arpeggios

Formula (R, ♭3, 5, ♭7, 9, 11)

Minor eleventh arpeggios are formed with the root, minor third, perfect fifth, minor seventh, major ninth and major eleventh. Using the CAGED system, below are five movable shapes that allow you to play the minor eleventh arpeggio all over the fretboard. These arpeggios sound great over minor, minor seventh, minor ninth, minor eleventh and minor thirteenth chords.

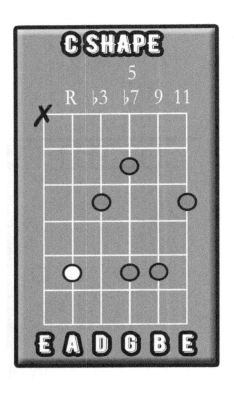

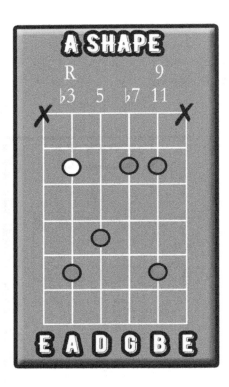

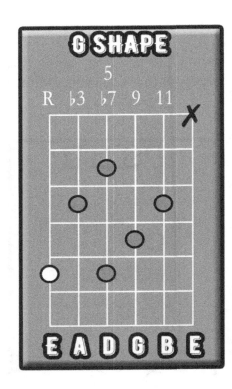

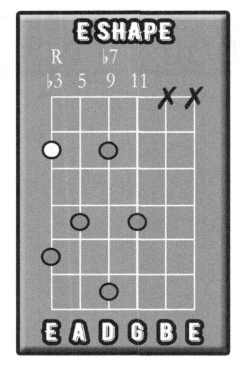

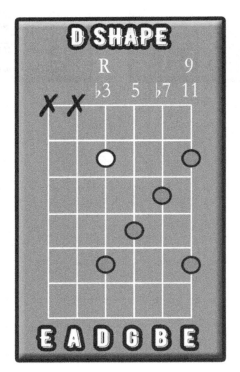

Practising Minor Eleventh Arpeggios

Below are some practice ideas to help learn each of the minor eleventh arpeggio CAGED shapes in the key of D. I recommend practising from the root note like the exercises below as this will help you move the shapes around more smoothly when changing key. Make sure you pay close attention to the picking strokes, hammer-ons and pull-offs, as well as the left-hand finger recommendations as this will help organise your fingers without moving position.

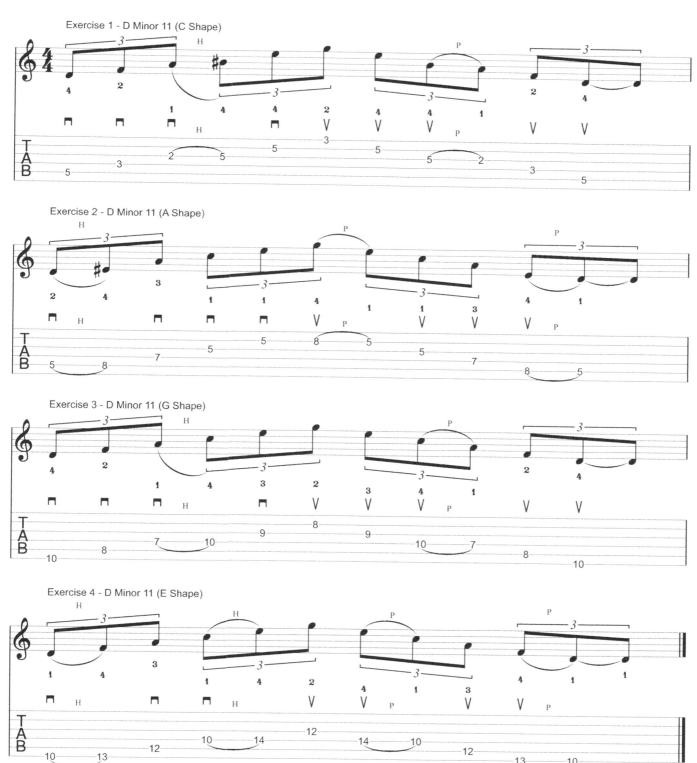

Exercise 5 - D Minor 11 (D Shape)

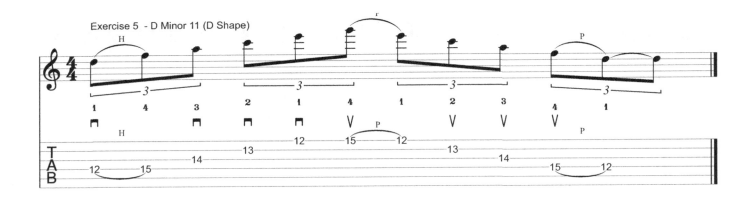

Dominant Eleventh Arpeggios

Formula (R, 3, 5, ♭7, 9, 11)

Dominant eleventh arpeggios are formed with the root, major third, perfect fifth, minor seventh, major ninth and major eleventh. Using the CAGED system, below are five movable shapes that allow you to play the dominant eleventh arpeggio all over the fretboard. These arpeggios sound great over dominant seventh, dominant ninth, dominant eleventh and dominant thirteenth chords.

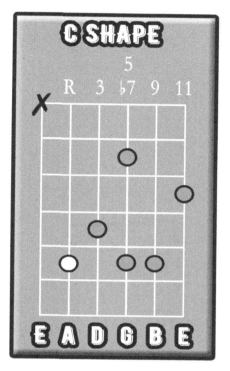

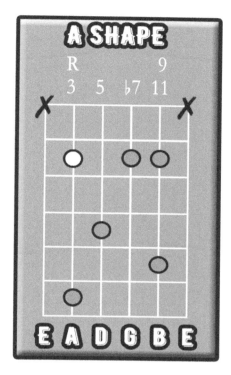

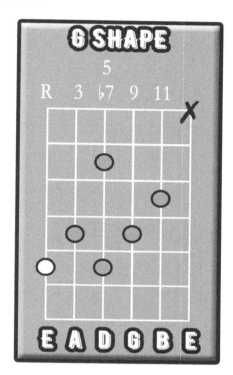

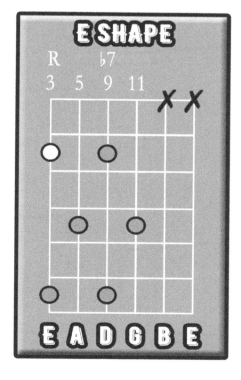

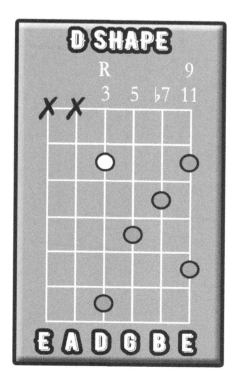

Practising Dominant Eleventh Arpeggios

Below are some practice ideas to help learn each of the dominant eleventh arpeggio CAGED shapes in the key of D. I recommend practising from the root note like the exercises below as this will help you move the shapes around more smoothly when changing key. Make sure you pay close attention to the picking strokes, hammer-ons and pull-offs, as well as the left-hand finger recommendations as this will help organise your fingers without moving position.

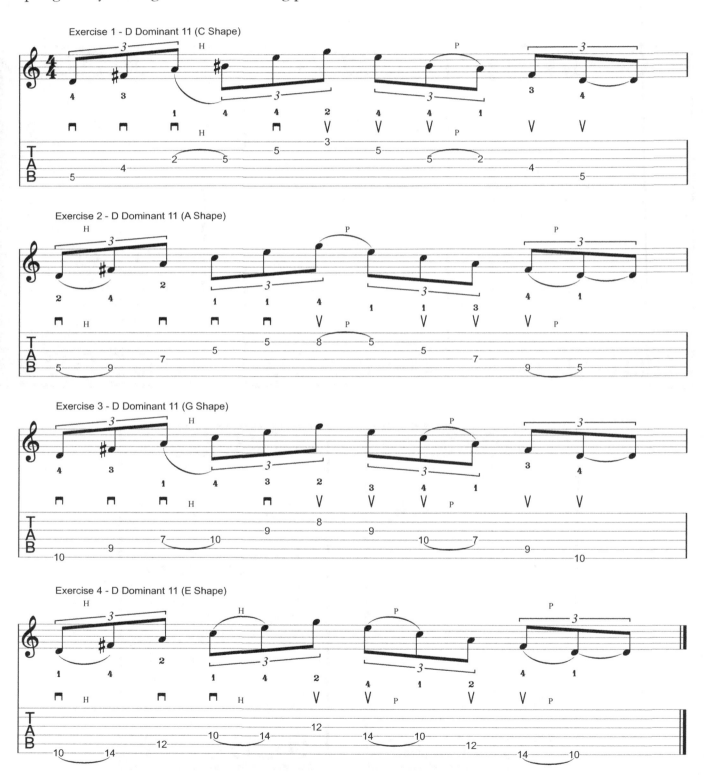

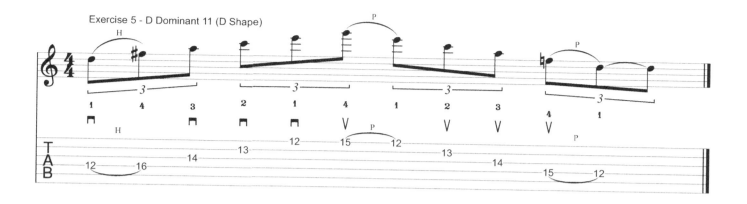

Exercise 5 - D Dominant 11 (D Shape)

Major Thirteenth Arpeggios
Formula (R, 3, 5, 7, 9, 11, 13)

Major thirteenth arpeggios are formed with the root, major third, perfect fifth, major seventh, major ninth, major eleventh and major thirteenth. The major thirteenth is actually a major sixth an octave up from the root. Using the CAGED system, below are five movable shapes that allow you to play the major eleventh arpeggios all over the fretboard. These arpeggios sound great over major, major seventh, major ninth, major eleventh and major thirteenth chords.

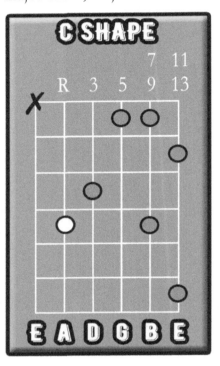

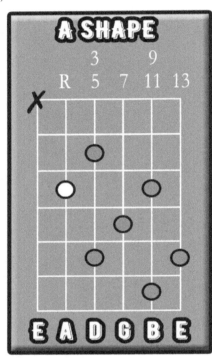

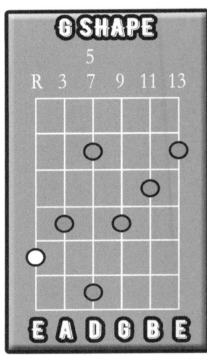

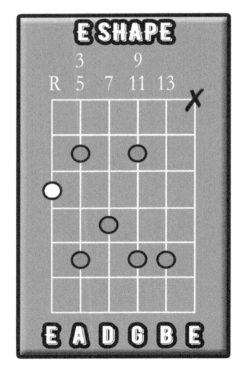

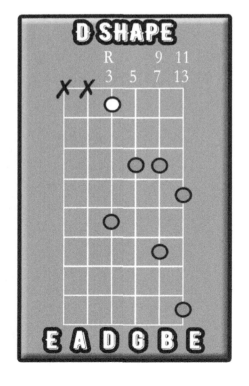

Practising Major Thirteenth Arpeggios

Below are some practice ideas to help learn each of the major thirteenth arpeggio CAGED shapes in the key of D. I recommend practising from the root note like the exercises below as this will help you move the shapes around more smoothly when changing key. Make sure you pay close attention to the picking strokes, hammer-ons and pull-offs as well as the left-hand finger recommendations as this will help organise your fingers without moving position.

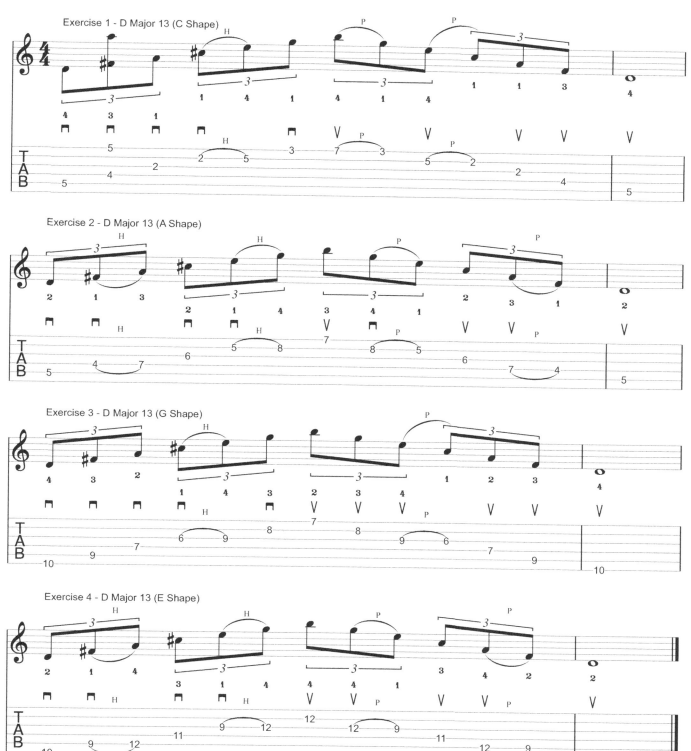

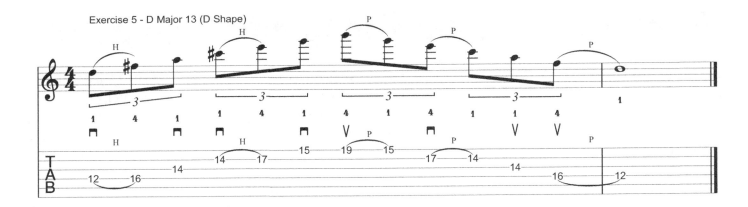

Exercise 5 - D Major 13 (D Shape)

Below are two alternative shapes that are very useful for the CAGED A and E major thirteenth arpeggio that you can experiment with as well:

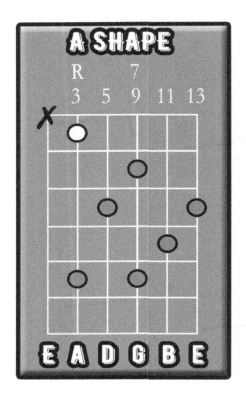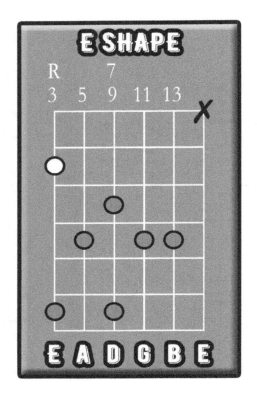

Minor Thirteenth Arpeggios

Formula (R, ♭3, 5, ♭7, 9, 11, 13)

Minor thirteenth arpeggios are formed with the root, minor third, perfect fifth, minor seventh, major ninth, major eleventh and major thirteenth. Using the CAGED system, below are five movable shapes that allow you to play the minor thirteenth arpeggios all over the fretboard. These arpeggios sound great over minor, minor seventh, minor ninth, minor eleventh and minor thirteenth chords.

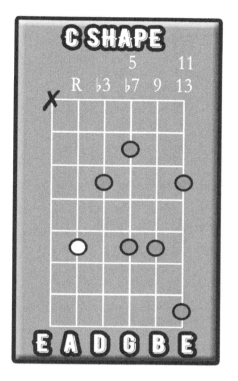

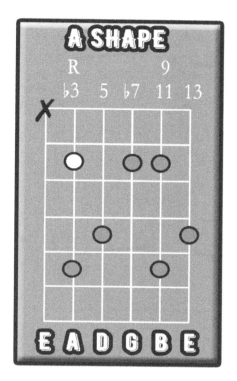

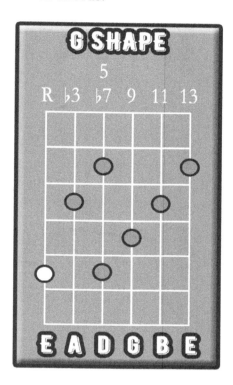

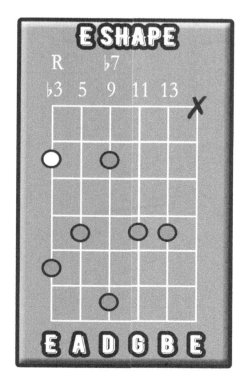

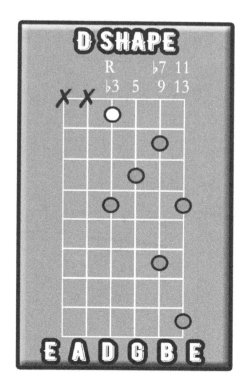

Practising Minor Thirteenth Arpeggios

Below are some practice ideas to help learn each of the minor thirteenth arpeggio CAGED shapes in the key of D. I recommend practising from the root note like the exercises below as this will help you move the shapes around more smoothly when changing key. Make sure you pay close attention to the picking strokes, hammer-ons and pull-offs, as well as the left-hand finger recommendations as this will help organise your fingers without moving position.

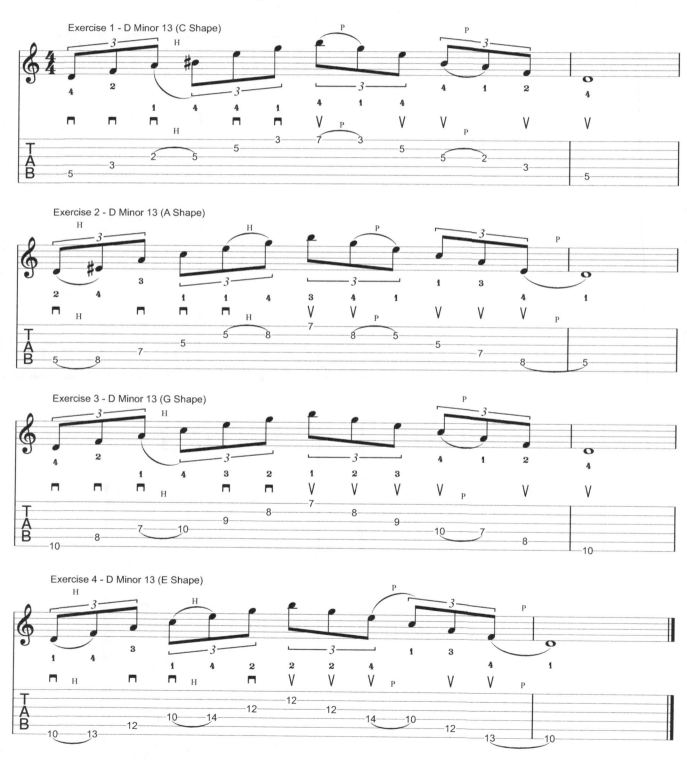

Exercise 5 - D Minor 13 (D Shape)

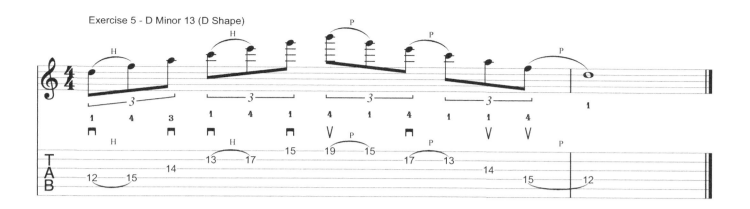

Dominant Thirteenth Arpeggios

Formula (R, 3, 5, ♭7, 9, 11, 13)

Dominant thirteenth arpeggios are formed with the root, major third, perfect fifth, minor seventh, major ninth, major eleventh and major thirteenth. Using the CAGED system, below are five movable shapes that allow you to play the dominant thirteenth arpeggios all over the fretboard. These arpeggios sound great over dominant seventh, dominant ninth, dominant eleventh and dominant thirteenth chords.

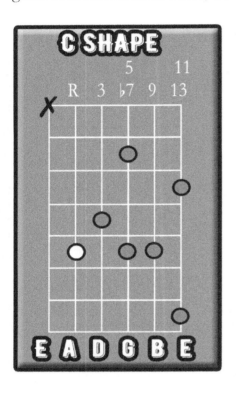

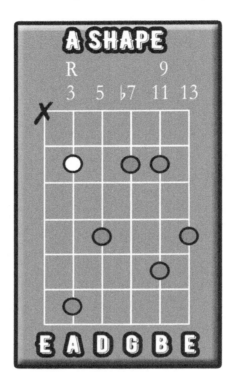

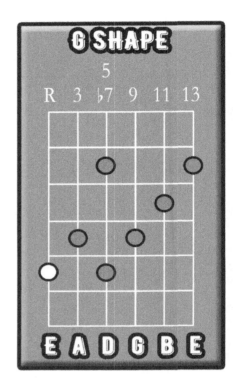

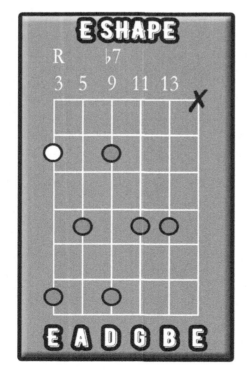

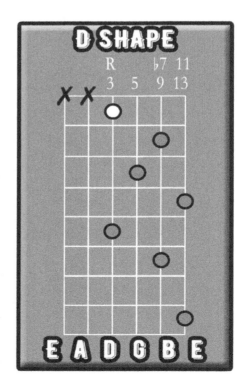

Practising Dominant Thirteenth Arpeggios

Below are some practice ideas to help learn each of the dominant thirteenth arpeggio CAGED shapes in the key of D. I recommend practising from the root note like the exercises below as this will help you move the shapes around more smoothly when changing key. Make sure you pay close attention to the picking strokes, hammer-ons and pull-offs, as well as the left-hand finger recommendations as this will help organise your fingers without moving position.

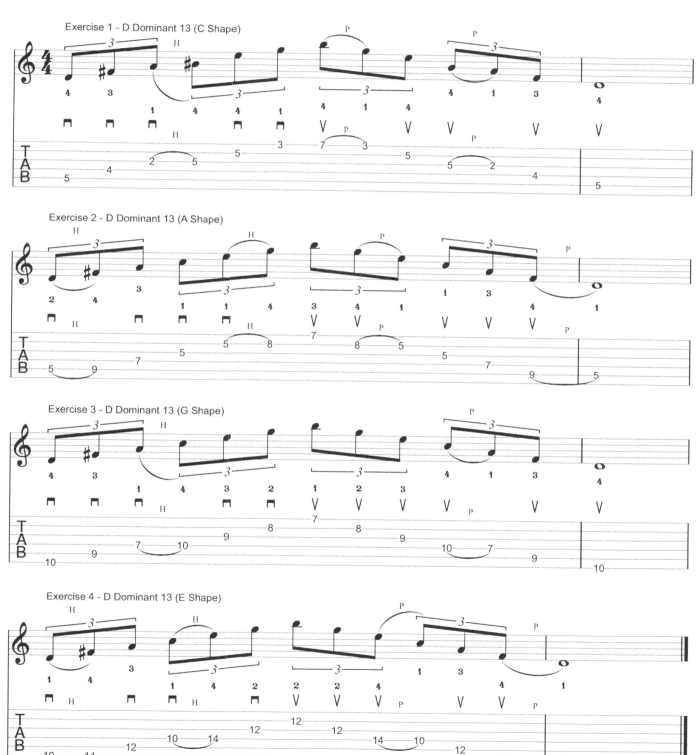

Exercise 5 - D Dominant 13 (D Shape)

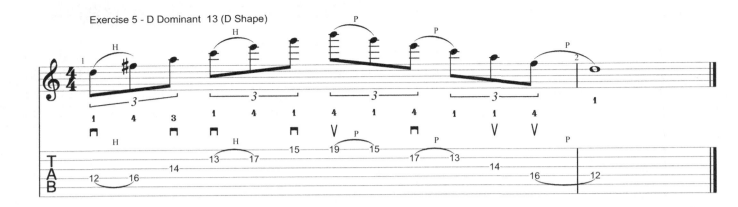

Keeping It Simple

A lot of the shapes in this book can be very intimidating. Sometimes when improvising it's a great idea just to take the basic major and minor triad arpeggio shapes and use them in small chunks, keeping it simple. Across the next few pages are arpeggio shapes that can be utilised over the three different string combinations for root position, first inversion and second inversion. I have added a fourth note to extend the shape for a turnaround. The shapes on the higher D to E strings are great for sweep picking.

MAJOR SHAPES

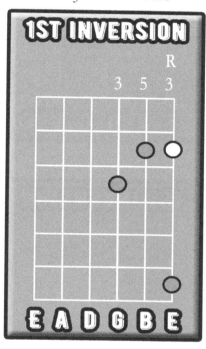
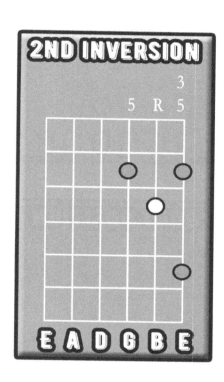

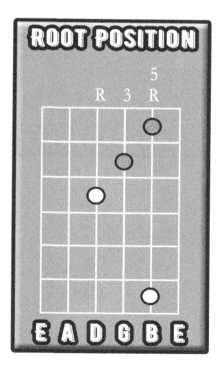
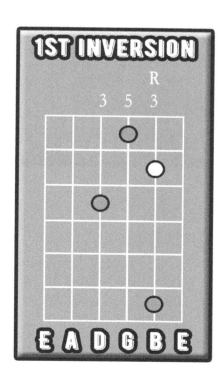
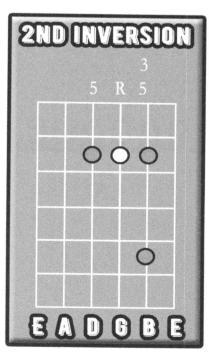

ROOT POSITION

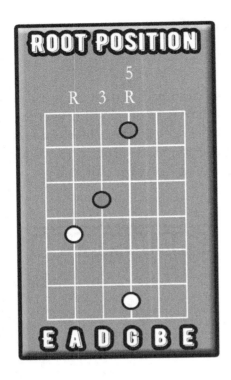

1ST INVERSION

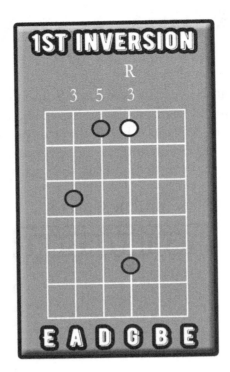

2ND INVERSION

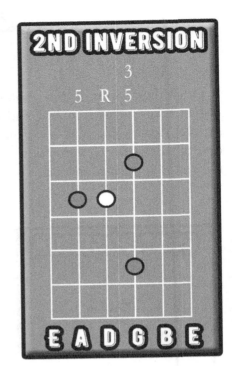

ROOT POSITION

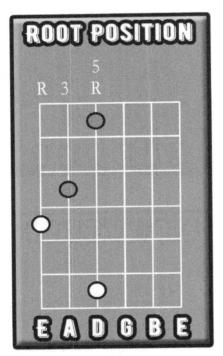

1ST INVERSION

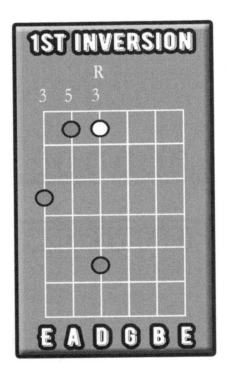

2ND INVERSION

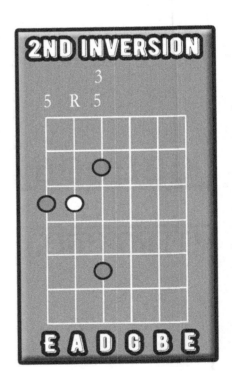

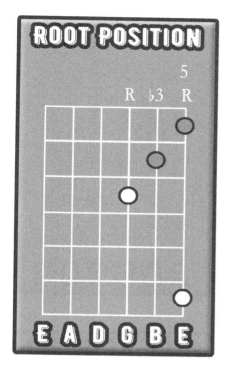

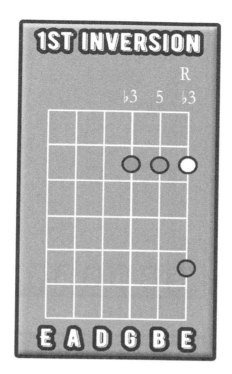

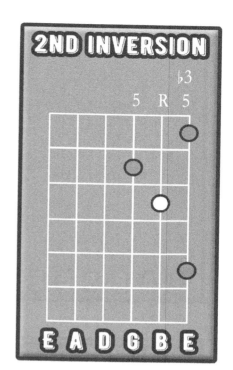

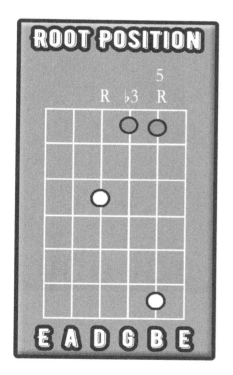

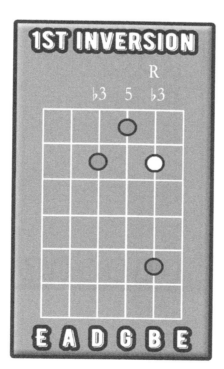

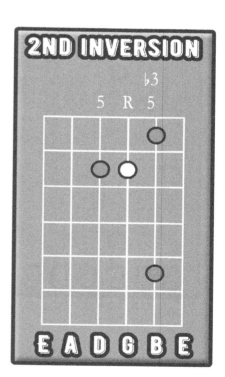

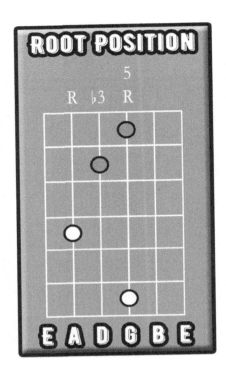

ROOT POSITION

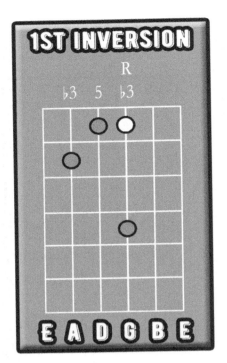

1ST INVERSION

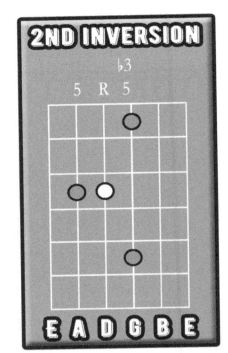

2ND INVERSION

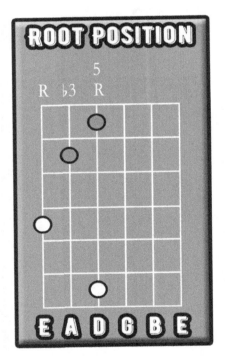

ROOT POSITION

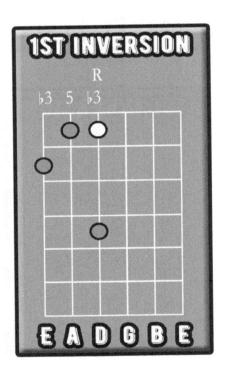

1ST INVERSION

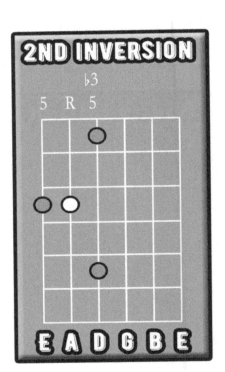

2ND INVERSION

82

Practising in One Position

Here are five useful shapes in the A position of the CAGED system for seventh chords. Practising in the order of major seven, dominant seven, minor seven, half-diminished and fully diminished is very logical as you only have to move one of the notes to create a new shape. When going from a major seven shape to a dominant seven shape you only need to flatten the seventh note, from a dominant shape to a minor seven shape you need to then flatten the third, from a minor seven to a half-diminished shape you flatten the fifth, and finally from a half-diminished to a fully-diminished shape you just need to flatten the seventh note again. You can apply this way of practising to all the shapes in this book for different CAGED shapes to help transition to different types of arpeggios.

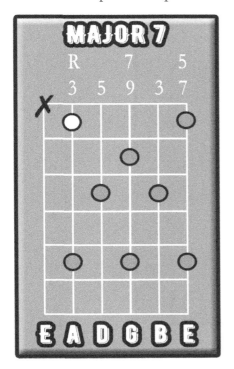

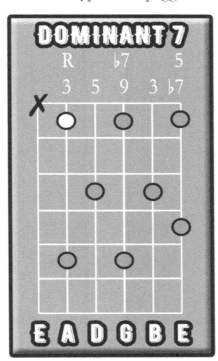

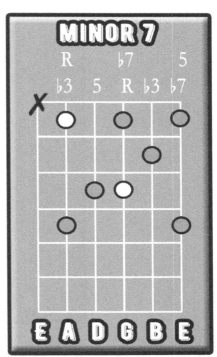

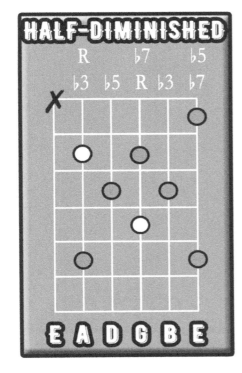

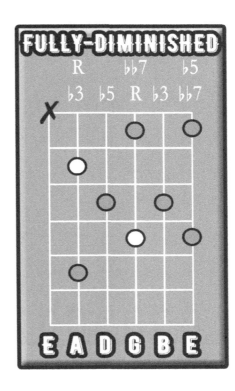

String Skipping Arpeggios

Other fun ways to incorporate arpeggios into your playing is by using string skipping, which was made popular by virtuoso guitarist Paul Gilbert. This helps avoid tricky shapes by playing the notes across strings with hammer-ons and pull-offs. Below are four useful shapes for basic triad arpeggios that are movable to any key on the higher four strings (D to high E string):

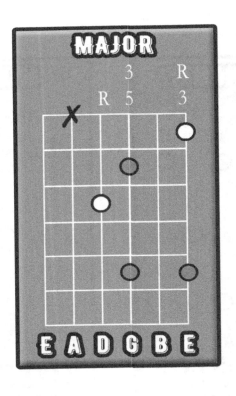

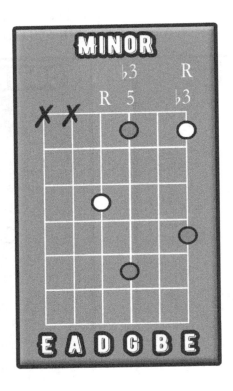

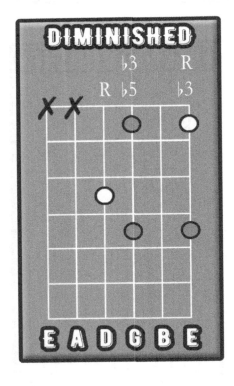

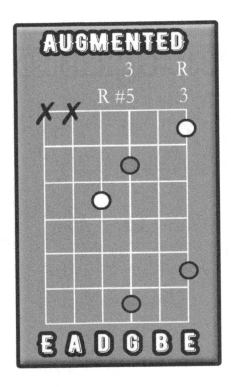

Here are some exercises in the key of D to help you to see how these shapes can be used, and also a great way to practice each shape. As with all exercises in this book, I recommend you use the circle of fifths to move and practice these shapes in all 12 keys.

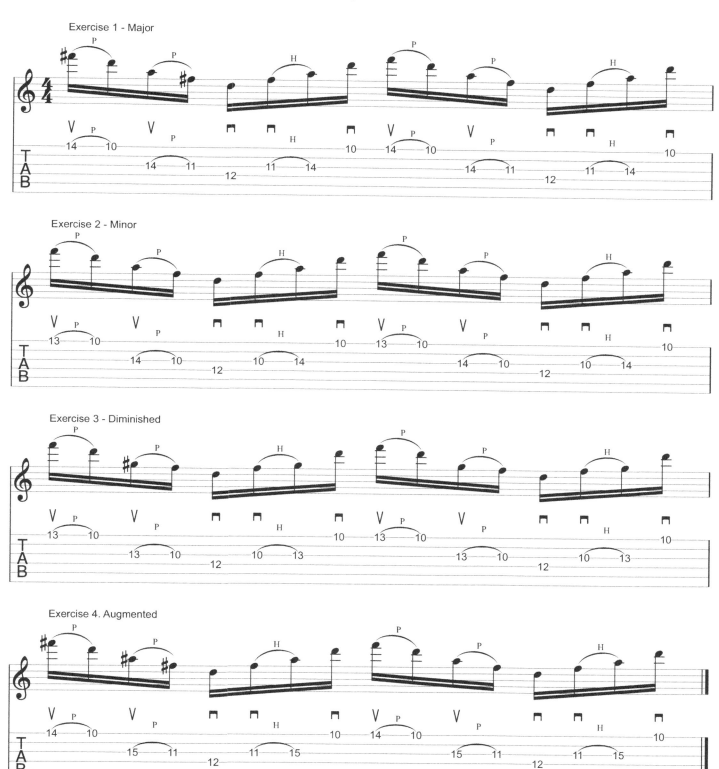

Below are four more useful shapes for basic triad arpeggios that are movable to any key on the middle four strings (A to B string). It is useful having shapes over different string combinations so you don't have to move far for your next shape.

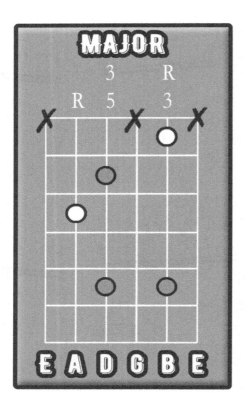

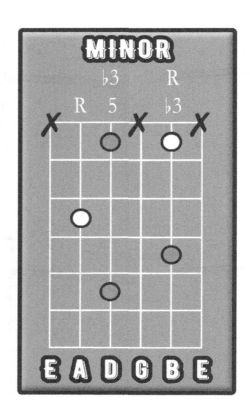

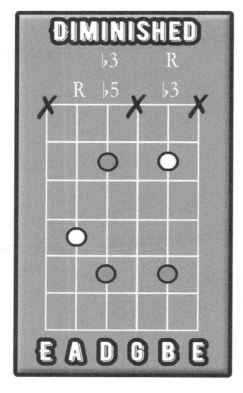

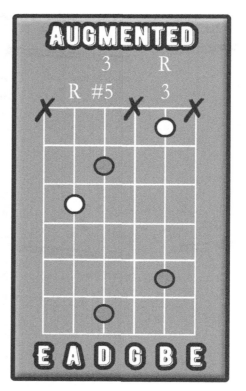

Here are some exercises in the key of D to help you see how these shapes can be used, but also they are a great way to practice each shape. As with all exercises in this book, I recommend you use the circle of fifths to move and practice these shapes in all 12 keys.

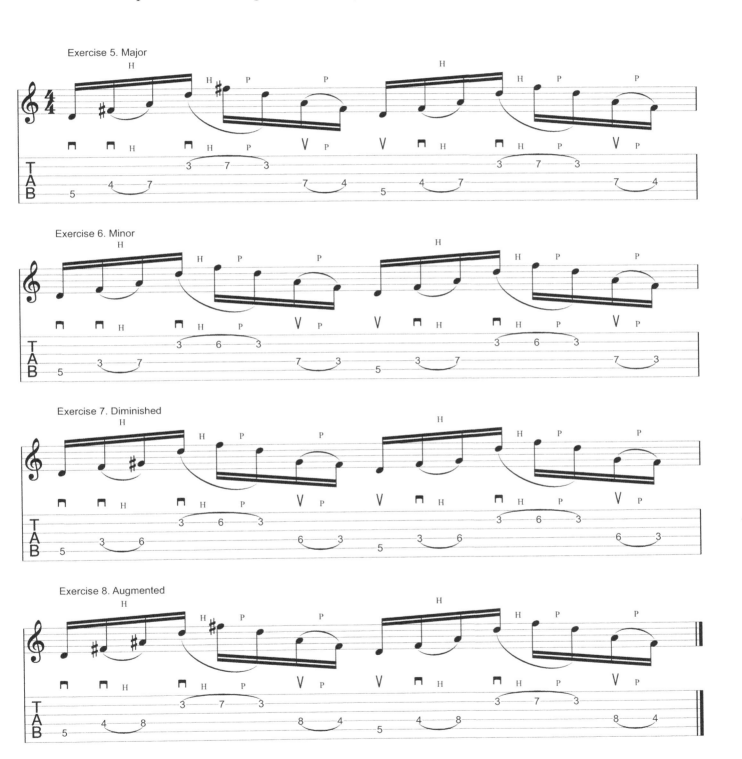

You can add the additional notes to create some very cool seventh string skipping arpeggios. Here are some example exercises below:

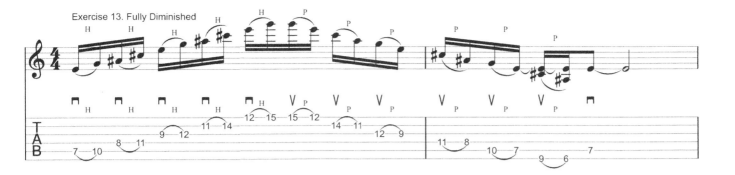

You can start adding more extended notes to create ninth, eleventh and thirteenth string skipping arpeggios, which can really help spice up your improvising skills.

Once you get comfortable with the shapes you can start experimenting with different note combinations of the arpeggios. Here are some examples below using basic triad arpeggios:

Tapped Arpeggio Ideas

A more advanced way of playing that allows you to play arpeggios on one string is tapping. Guthrie Govan often uses this technique in his playing and song arrangements. Below are some exercises in the key of E that show you how to play the basic triad arpeggios on one string, combining string skipping to move the same shape up two octaves and back down. These are very cool but not very easy to get under your fingers!

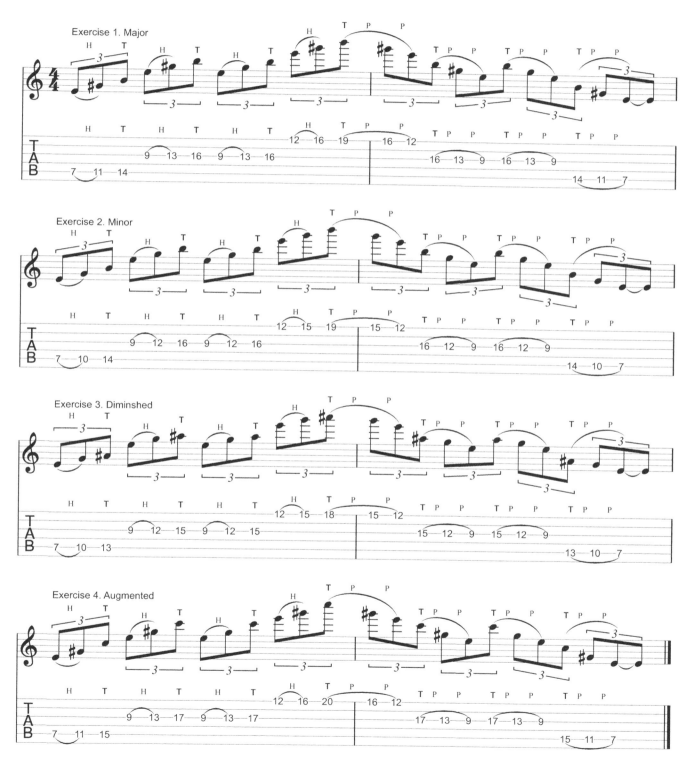

The exercises below take the same concept of tapping the full arpeggios on one string across octaves, but to the seventh degree. These sound killer but are very hard to play. Once again in the key of E:

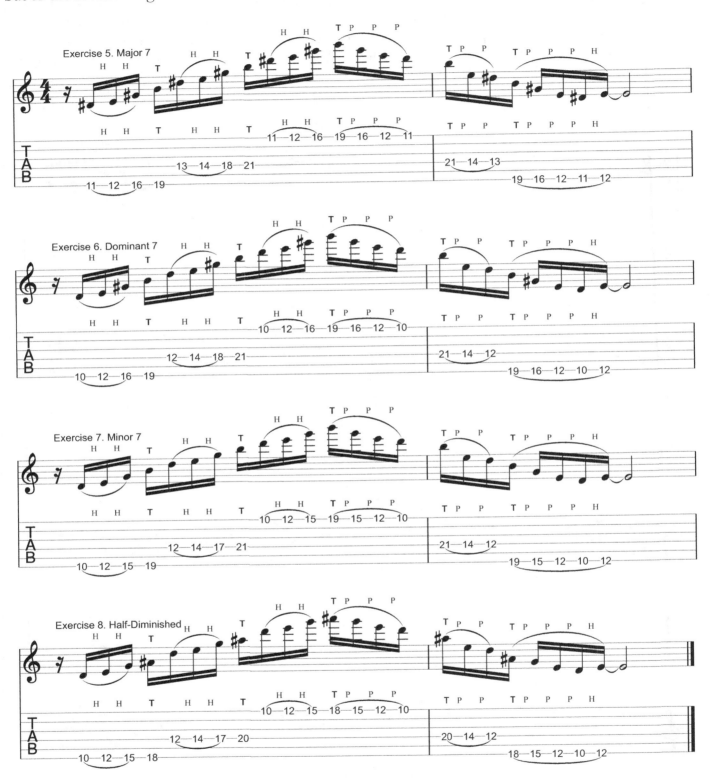

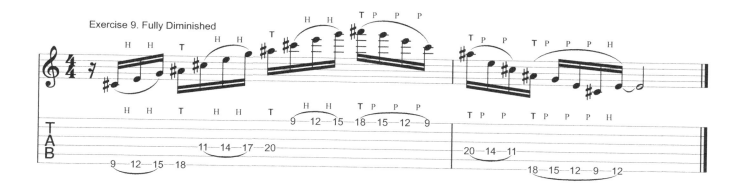

Exercise 9. Fully Diminished

Sweep Picking & Tapped Arpeggios

Here are some exercises using basic triad arpeggios and combining sweep picking patterns with some tapping over the 3, 4, 5 and 6 strings. You will find it easier to sweep and tap over the first four exercises, which are played over only three strings, and as you progress to exercises 13 to 16, where you are playing over all 6 strings, it becomes a bit more challenging.

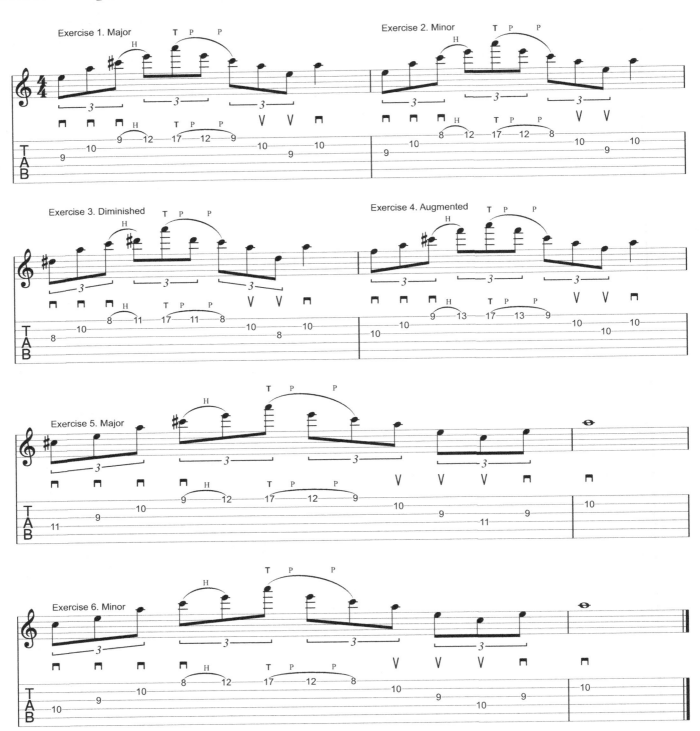

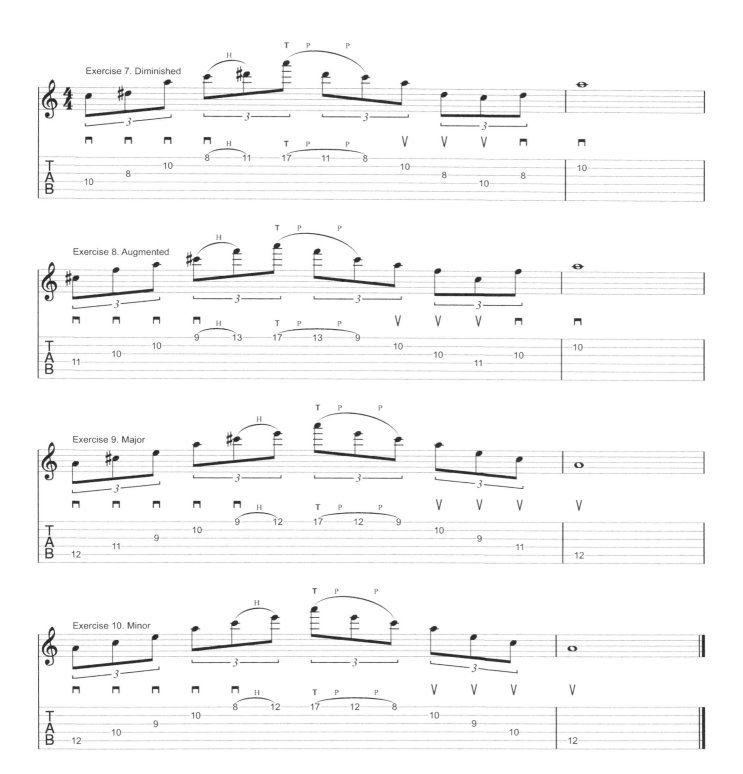

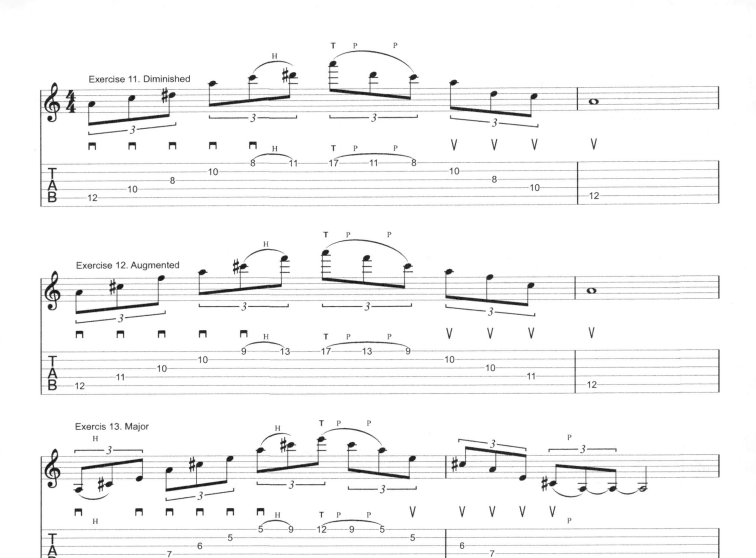

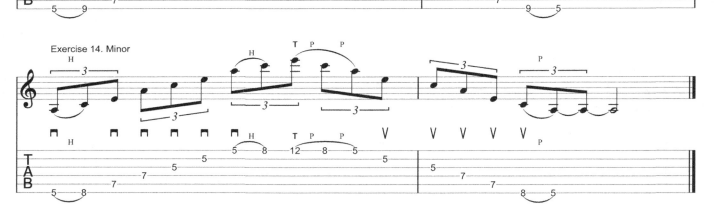

96

Horizontal and Diagonal Arpeggios

Horizontal Playing

Vertical Playing

Diagonal Playing

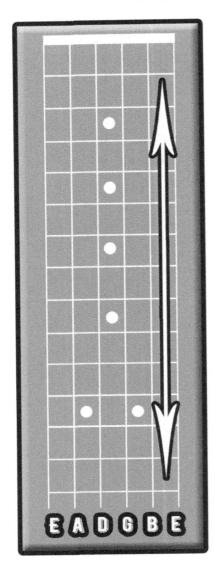
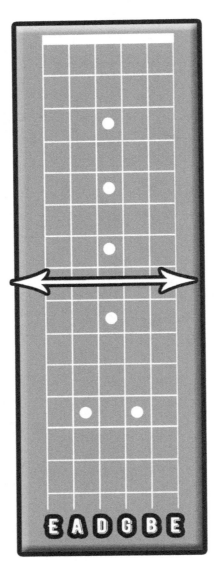
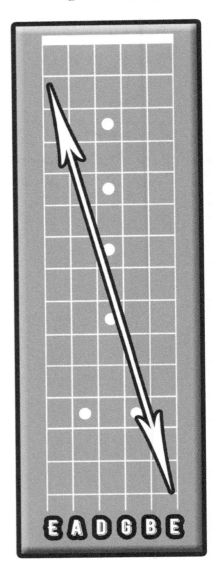

Most ideas in this book so far have been locked in vertical positions (from the perspective of the guitar player). We are now going to explore some horizontal and diagonal arpeggio ideas using seventh arpeggios in the key of A.

Exercises 1-3 – Here we explore moving the arpeggios on two string combinations horizontally across the fretboard starting on the low E and A strings, then onto the D and G strings, and finally onto the B and high E strings. You can alternate pick these or use legato.

Exercises 4-6 – Here we explore playing diagonally over the fretboard with four and six string combinations.

MAJOR 7 ARPEGGIOS

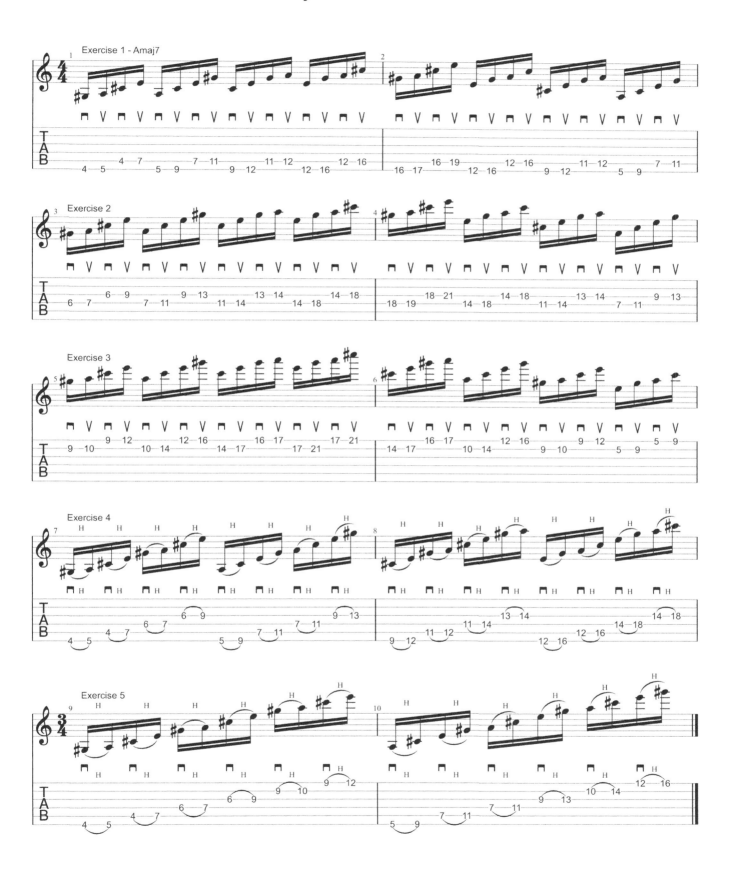

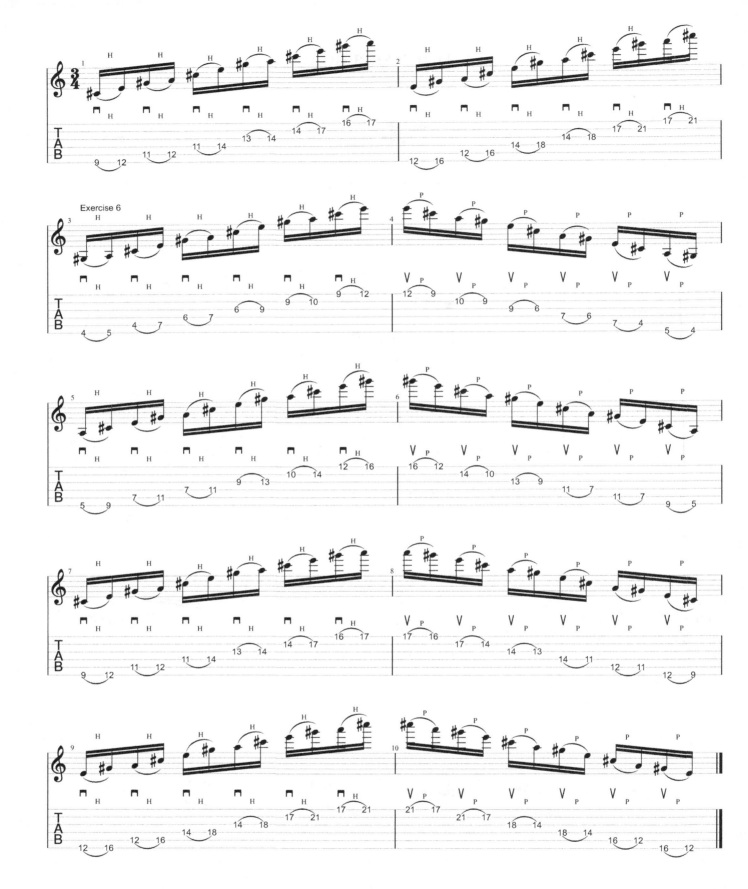

MINOR 7 ARPEGGIOS

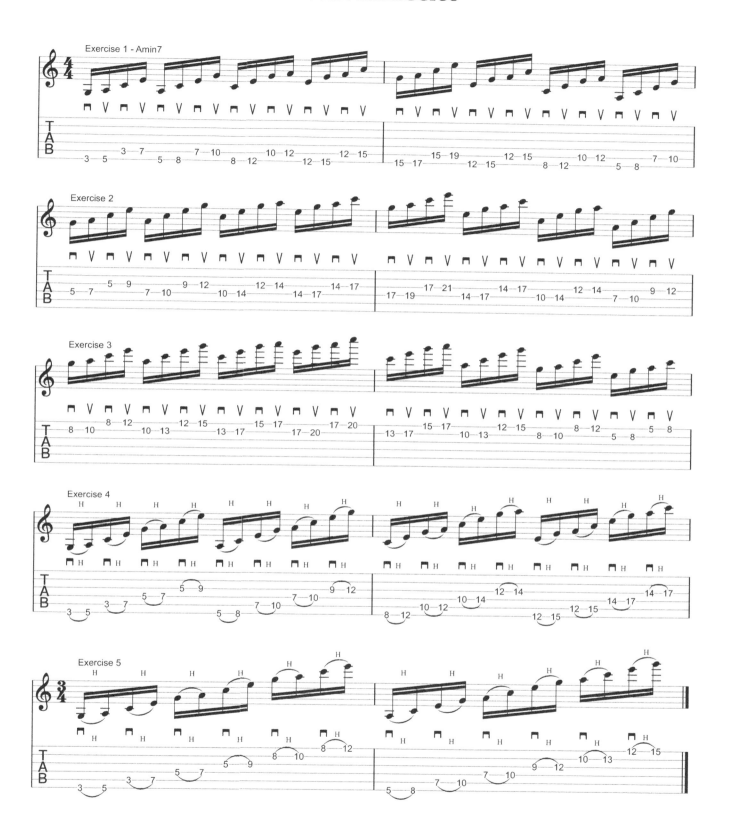

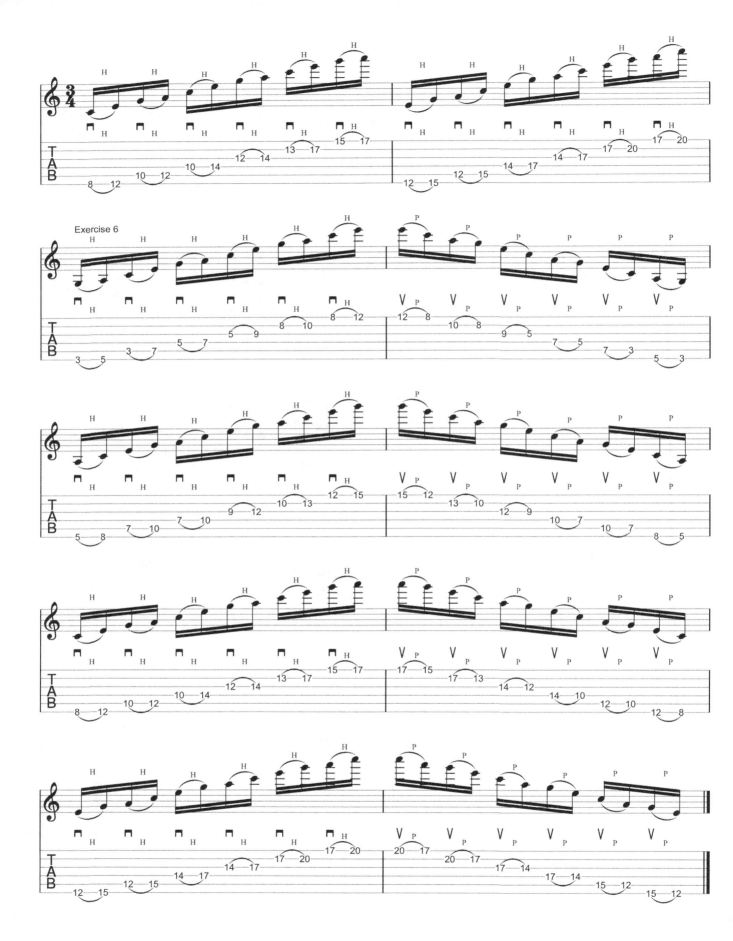

102

DOMINANT 7 ARPEGGIOS

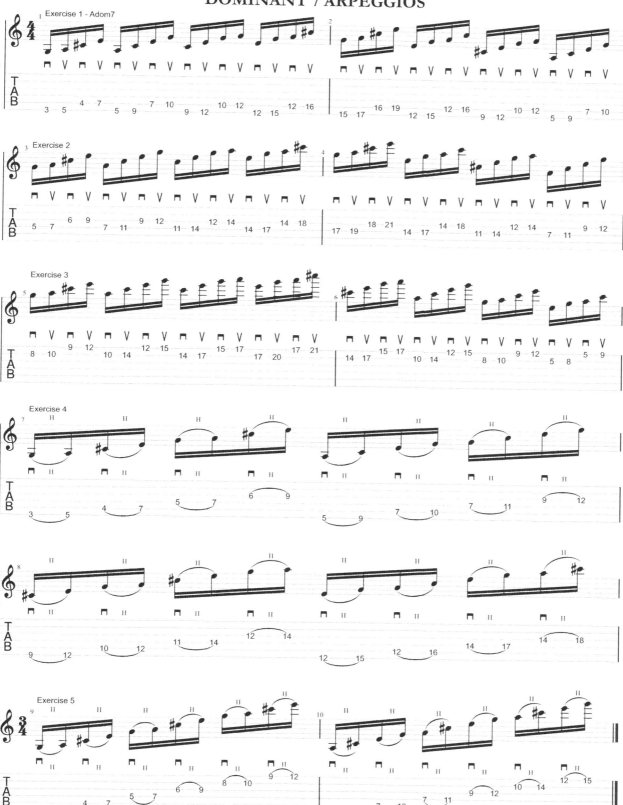

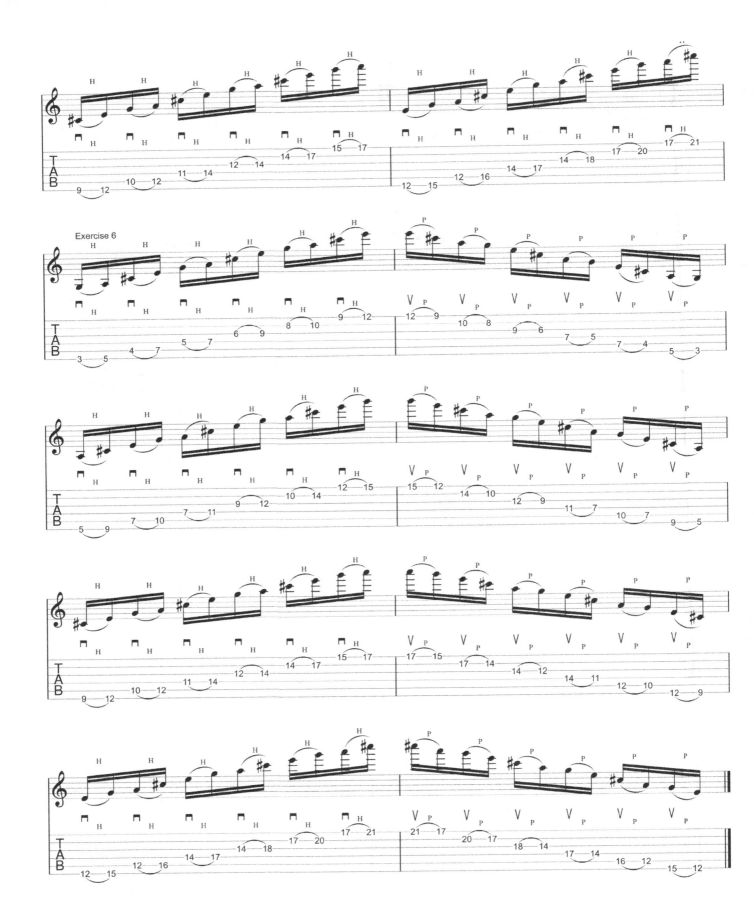

HALF-DIMINISHED ARPEGGIOS

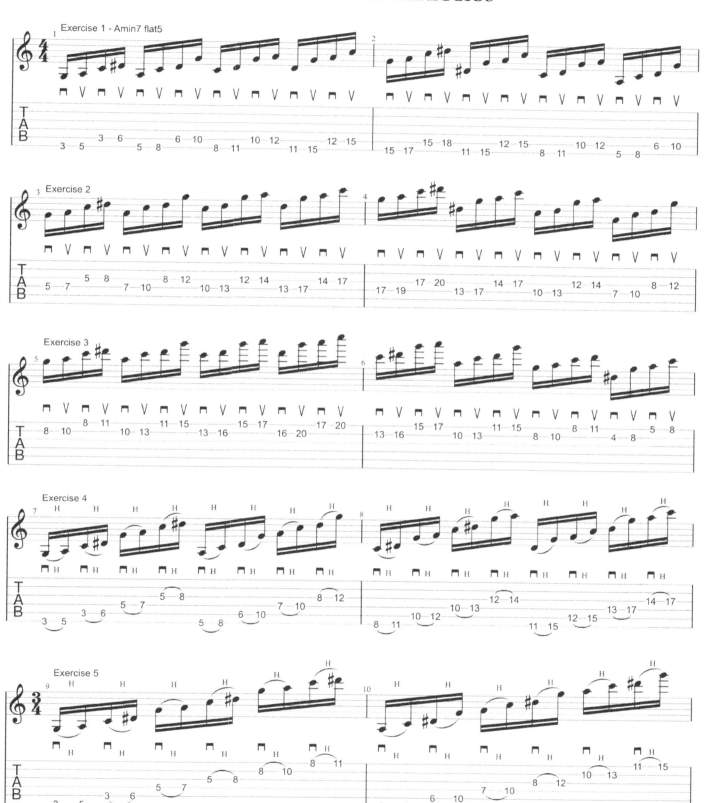

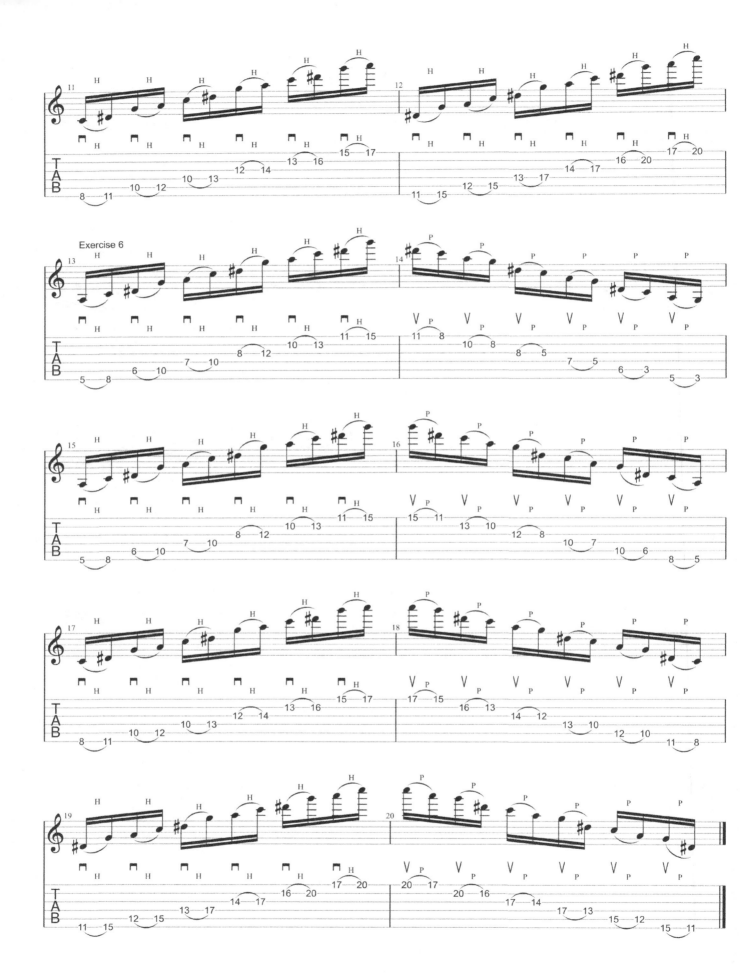

FULLY-DIMINISHED ARPEGGIOS

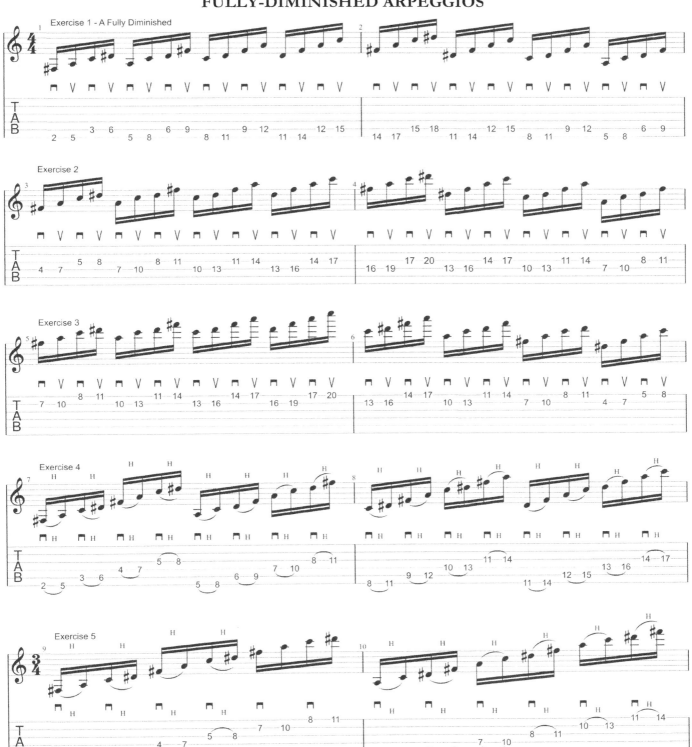

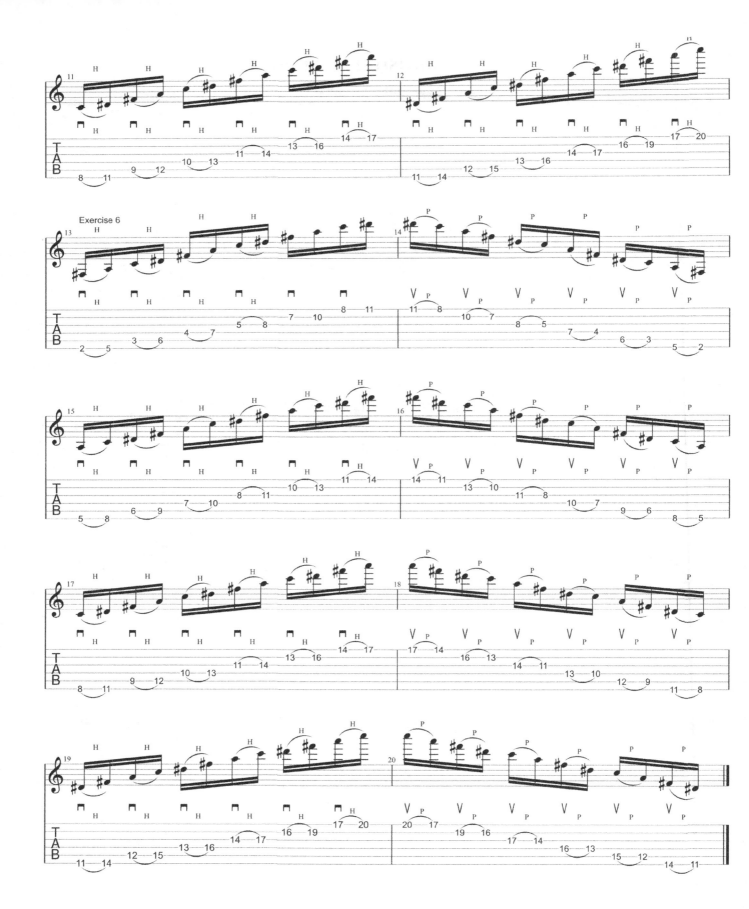

108

What Is The CAGED System?

The idea of the CAGED system is that you can find any scale, chord, or arpeggio within five or six frets and keep your hand in one position. In this example we will look at the basic major chords, major arpeggios and major scale showing how they connect over the entire fretboard. Hopefully this will help you see how you can apply this to all the arpeggios in this book. You do not need to understand this to practice the shapes, but it helps!

Let's first take the five basic open major chords **C**, **A**, **G**, **E** and **D**. We want to then link all these basic shapes across the whole fretboard. This then creates every possible shape to play C major. You will need to bar the shapes to recreate the open strings. Once you reach the D shape you will be connected to the C shape again, an octave up, and then the same patterns repeat until you run out of frets.

For every type of chord, arpeggio, and scale, there are five shapes you can connect together.

The next step is to connect the CAGED major scale shaped around these chords.

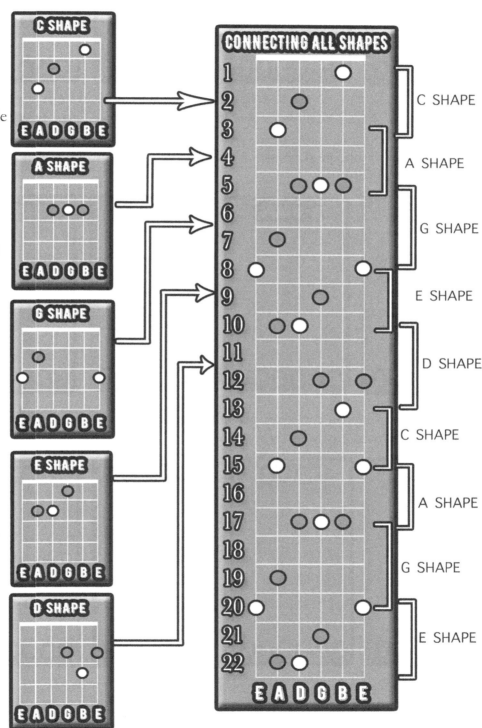

Taking our five CAGED major scale shapes, you should now see within them the five CAGED major chord shapes (highlighted below):

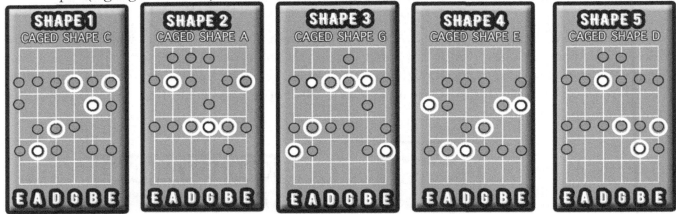

This same method can be applied to any of the CAGED system scales. You just have to learn the CAGED chord shapes that work for that particular scale. For example, with the harmonic minor CAGED shapes, after learning all five CAGED shapes for minor-major seventh chords you will see that these chords are embedded in the CAGED shapes. You can even build them yourself using the appropriate chord formulas.

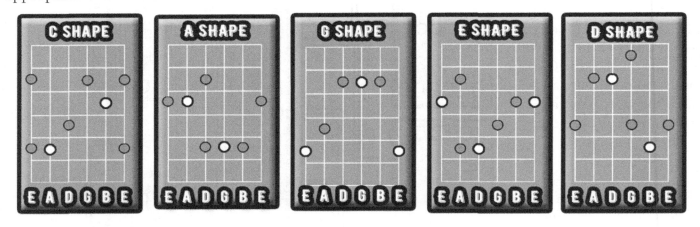

As mentioned earlier you can even play all your arpeggios within the CAGED shapes. Here are all five CAGED major arpeggios:

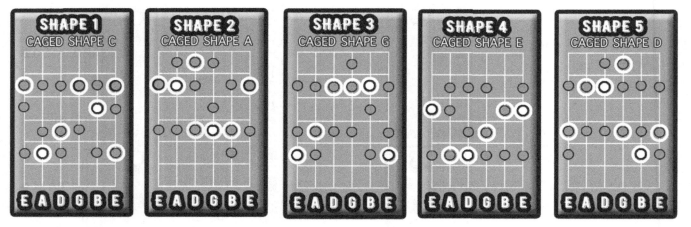

Notice above in the major CAGED scales the embedded chords and arpeggios. This is why the CAGED system is so helpful in connecting the fretboard.

Vising **www.karlgolden.org/CAGEDSystem** for a video masterclass on the CAGED system.

Circle Of Fourths & Fifths

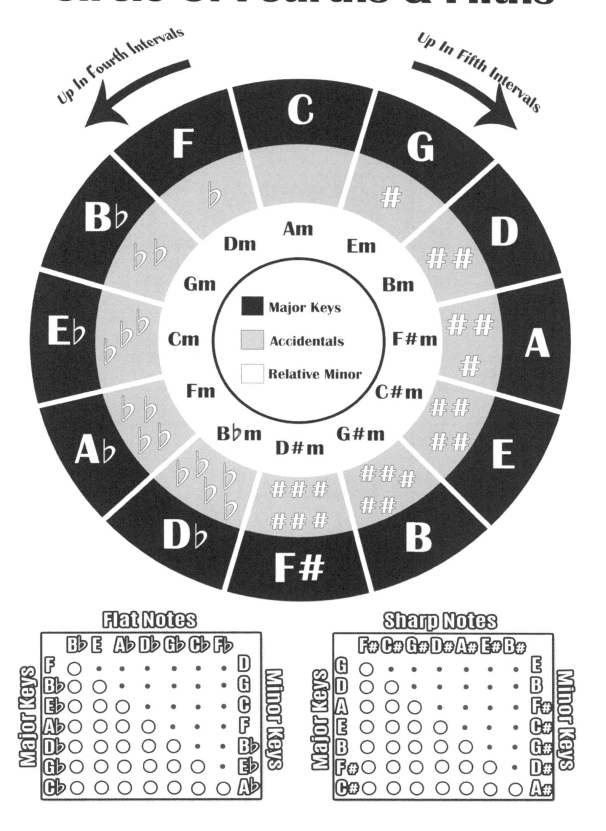

The circle of fourths and fifths is a great way to practice the arpeggio shapes in this book in every key. Start with C and make your way round clockwise through the 12 keys when using the circle of fifths.

Creating Your Own Shapes

Over the next few pages are some empty charts and blank tablature where you can create your own shapes or make some alterations to the shapes in this book.

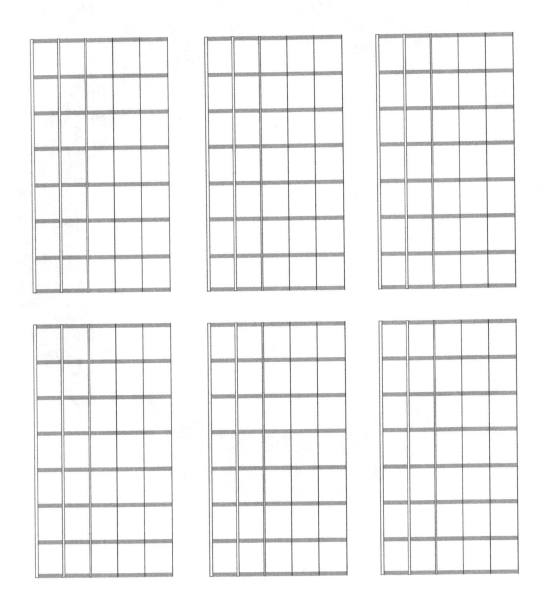

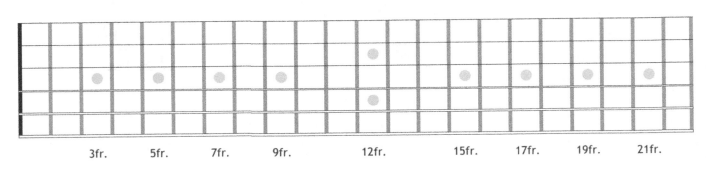

| | 3fr. | 5fr. | 7fr. | 9fr. | 12fr. | 15fr. | 17fr. | 19fr. | 21fr. |

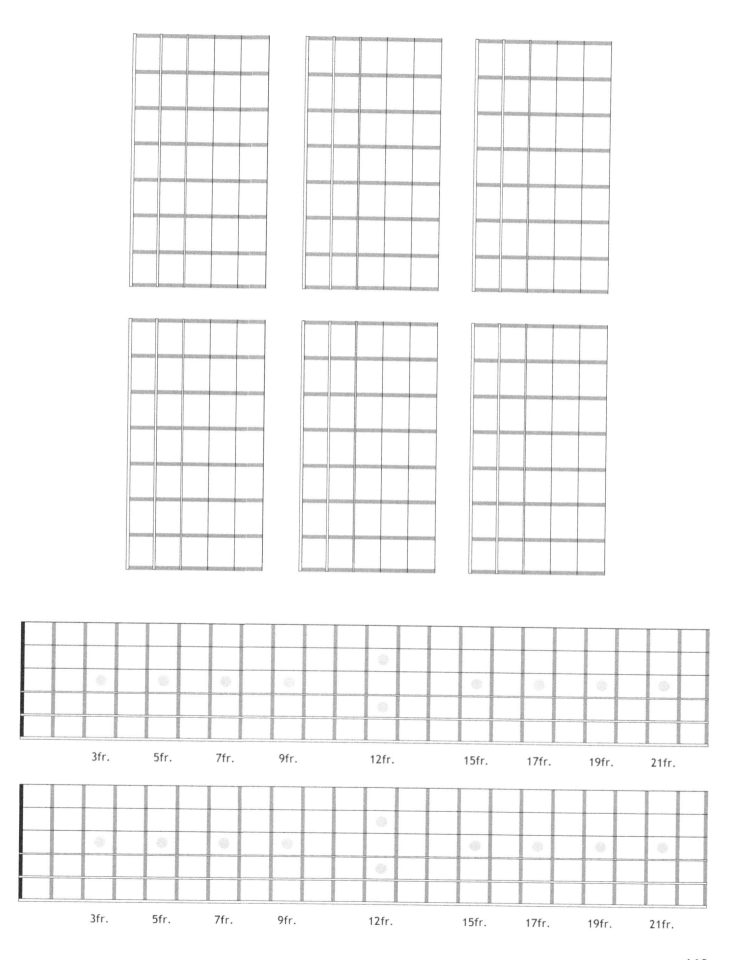

3fr.   5fr.   7fr.   9fr.   12fr.   15fr.   17fr.   19fr.   21fr.

3fr.   5fr.   7fr.   9fr.   12fr.   15fr.   17fr.   19fr.   21fr.

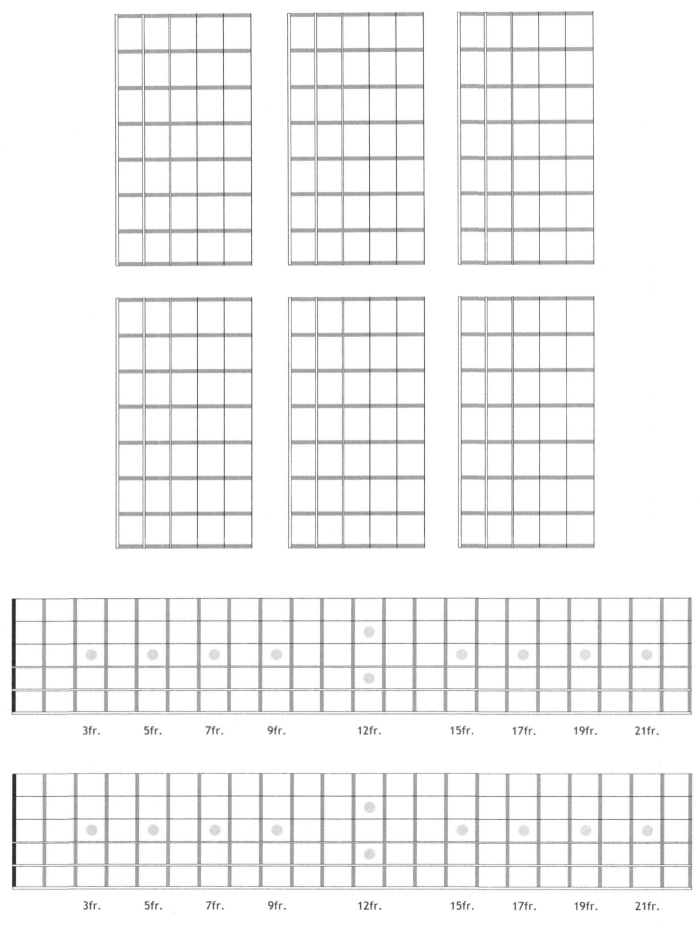

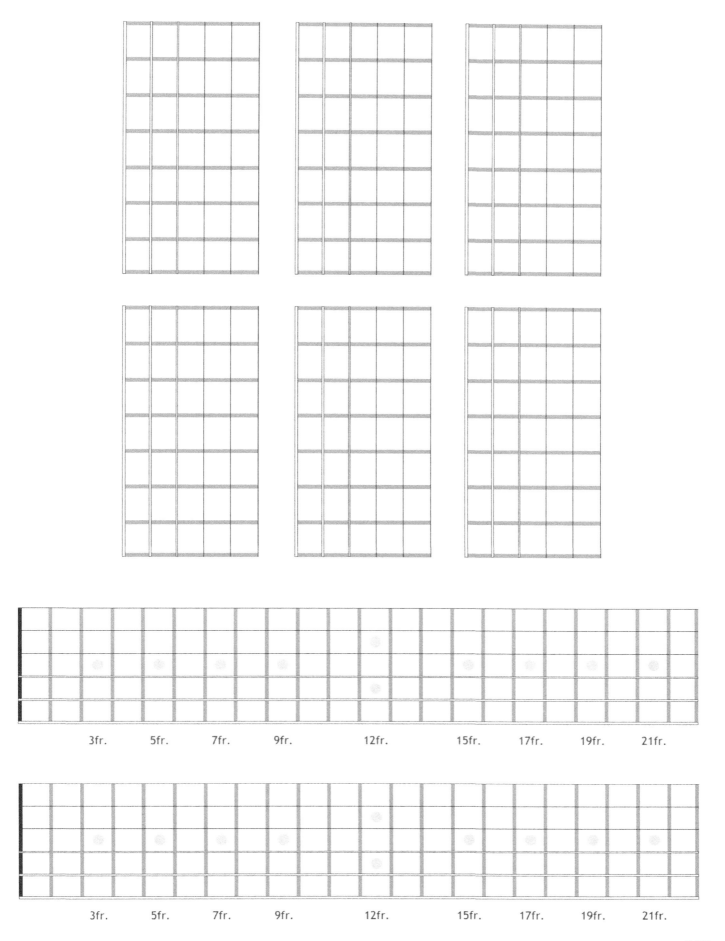

3fr. 5fr. 7fr. 9fr. 12fr. 15fr. 17fr. 19fr. 21fr.

3fr. 5fr. 7fr. 9fr. 12fr. 15fr. 17fr. 19fr. 21fr.

Practice Diary

It is very important to maintain a good practice routine by keeping track of your goals and progress. By doing this you can feel a real sense of achievement and look back on how far you have progressed. I recommend keeping track of what shapes you have learned and what you have discovered.

Week: _____

Goals This Week:

_____

_____

_____

_____

Achievements This Week:

_____

_____

_____

_____

Things To Work On Next Week:

_____

_____

_____

_____

Notes:

_____

_____

_____

_____

Week: _____

Goals This Week:

_____

_____

_____

_____

Achievements This Week:

_____

_____

_____

_____

Things To Work On Next Week:

_____

_____

_____

_____

Notes:

_____

_____

_____

_____

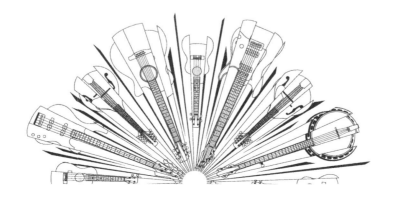

Week: _____

Goals This Week:

_____

_____

_____

_____

Achievements This Week:

_____

_____

_____

_____

Things To Work On Next Week:

_____

_____

_____

_____

Notes:

_____

_____

_____

_____

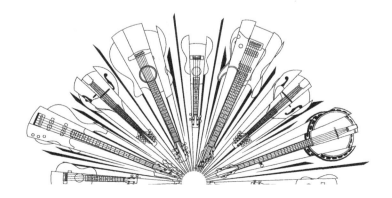

Week: _____

Goals This Week:

_____
_____
_____
_____

Achievements This Week:

_____
_____
_____
_____

Things To Work On Next Week:

_____
_____
_____
_____

Notes:

_____
_____
_____
_____

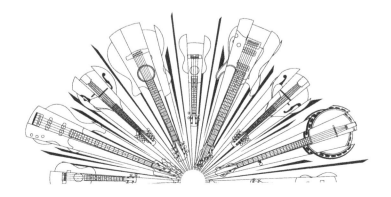

Week: _____

Goals This Week:

_____

_____

_____

_____

Achievements This Week:

_____

_____

_____

_____

Things To Work On Next Week:

_____

_____

_____

_____

Notes:

_____

_____

_____

_____

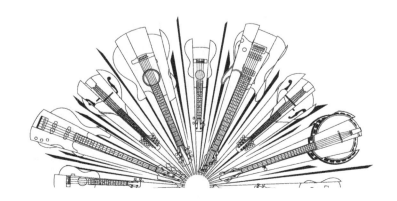

Week: _____

Goals This Week:

_____

_____

_____

_____

Achievements This Week:

_____

_____

_____

_____

Things To Work On Next Week:

_____

_____

_____

_____

Notes:

_____

_____

_____

_____

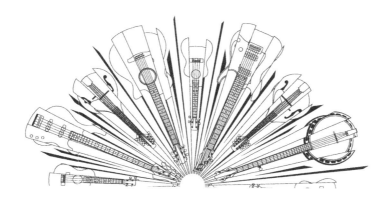

Week: _____

Goals This Week:

_____
_____
_____
_____

Achievements This Week:

_____
_____
_____
_____

Things To Work On Next Week:

_____
_____
_____
_____

Notes:

_____
_____
_____
_____

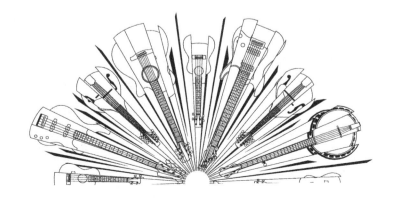

Week: _____

Goals This Week:

_____
_____
_____
_____

Achievements This Week:

_____
_____
_____
_____

Things To Work On Next Week:

_____
_____
_____
_____

Notes:

_____
_____
_____
_____

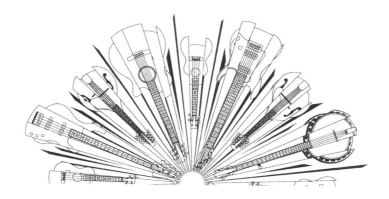

Week: _____

Goals This Week:

_____
_____
_____
_____

Achievements This Week:

_____
_____
_____
_____

Things To Work On Next Week:

_____
_____
_____
_____

Notes:

_____
_____
_____
_____

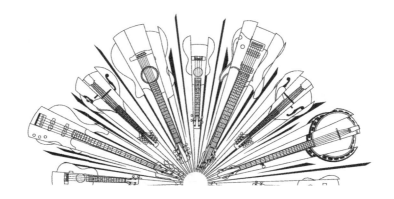

Week: _____

Goals This Week:

_____

_____

_____

_____

Achievements This Week:

_____

_____

_____

_____

Things To Work On Next Week:

_____

_____

_____

_____

Notes:

_____

_____

_____

_____

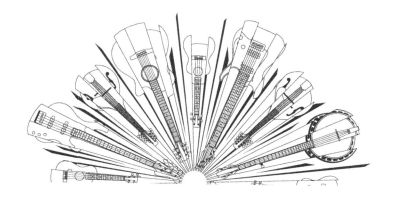

Week: _____

Goals This Week:

_____
_____
_____
_____

Achievements This Week:

_____
_____
_____
_____

Things To Work On Next Week:

_____
_____
_____
_____

Notes:

_____
_____
_____
_____

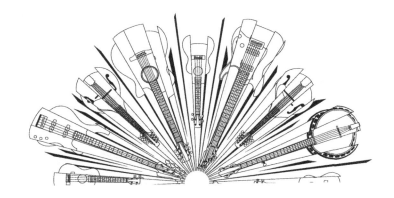

Week: _____

Goals This Week:

_____

_____

_____

_____

Achievements This Week:

_____

_____

_____

_____

Things To Work On Next Week:

_____

_____

_____

_____

Notes:

_____

_____

_____

_____

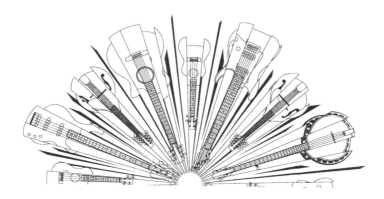

Week: _____

Goals This Week:

_____
_____
_____
_____

Achievements This Week:

_____
_____
_____
_____

Things To Work On Next Week:

_____
_____
_____
_____

Notes:

_____
_____
_____
_____

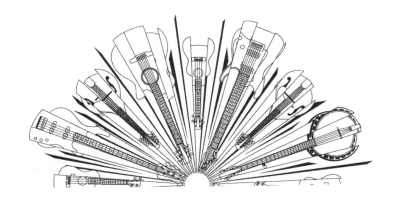

Week: _____

Goals This Week:

_____
_____
_____
_____

Achievements This Week:

_____
_____
_____
_____

Things To Work On Next Week:

_____
_____
_____
_____

Notes:

_____
_____
_____
_____

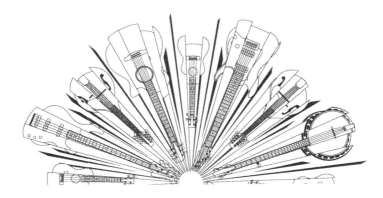

Week: _____

Goals This Week:

_____

_____

_____

_____

Achievements This Week:

_____

_____

_____

_____

Things To Work On Next Week:

_____

_____

_____

_____

Notes:

_____

_____

_____

_____

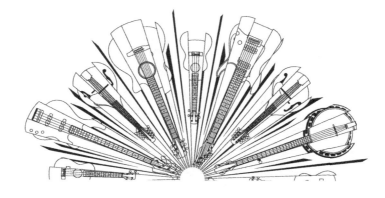

Week: _____

Goals This Week:

_____
_____
_____
_____

Achievements This Week:

_____
_____
_____
_____

Things To Work On Next Week:

_____
_____
_____
_____

Notes:

_____
_____
_____
_____

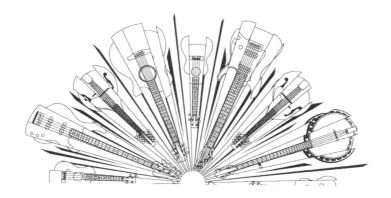

Week: _____

Goals This Week:

_____

_____

_____

_____

Achievements This Week:

_____

_____

_____

_____

Things To Work On Next Week:

_____

_____

_____

_____

Notes:

_____

_____

_____

_____

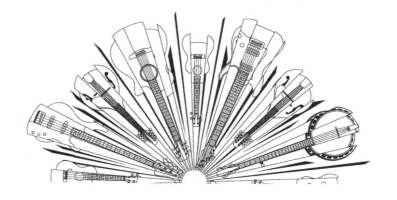

Week: _____

Goals This Week:

_____

_____

_____

_____

Achievements This Week:

_____

_____

_____

_____

Things To Work On Next Week:

_____

_____

_____

_____

Notes:

_____

_____

_____

_____

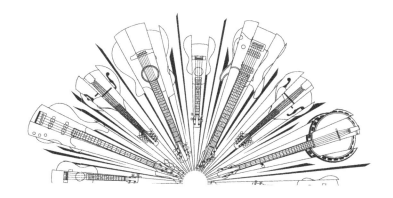

Week: _____

Goals This Week:

_____

_____

_____

_____

Achievements This Week:

_____

_____

_____

_____

Things To Work On Next Week:

_____

_____

_____

_____

Notes:

_____

_____

_____

_____

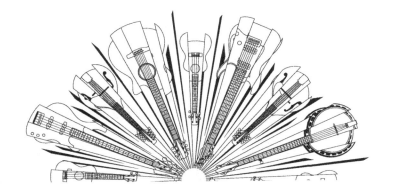

Week: _____

Goals This Week:

_____
_____
_____
_____

Achievements This Week:

_____
_____
_____
_____

Things To Work On Next Week:

_____
_____
_____
_____

Notes:

_____
_____
_____
_____

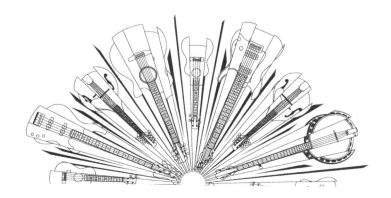

Week: _____

Goals This Week:

_____

_____

_____

_____

Achievements This Week:

_____

_____

_____

_____

Things To Work On Next Week:

_____

_____

_____

_____

Notes:

_____

_____

_____

_____

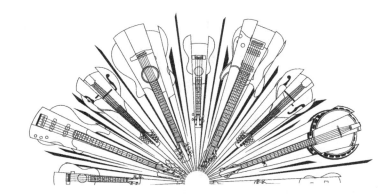

Week: _____

Goals This Week:

_____

_____

_____

_____

Achievements This Week:

_____

_____

_____

_____

Things To Work On Next Week:

_____

_____

_____

_____

Notes:

_____

_____

_____

_____

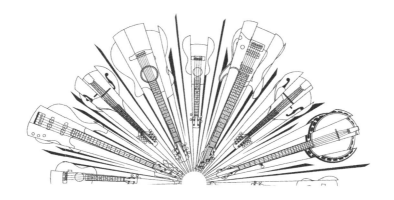

The Ultimate Guitar Series

Don't forget to check out the other books in 'The Ultimate Guitar Series'. You can also purchase my online video courses from **www.karlgolden.org/courses**

-The Ultimate Guitar Scales Book-

Going from the simplest scales, such as the Minor Pentatonic scale, through to the more complex, such as Harmonic Minor and Melodic Minor scales, this book uses 3-note per string and CAGED shapes to connect the different shapes across the whole fretboard. This book can be used simply as a reference point for shapes to play for certain scales/modes, or to further develop your knowledge and practice routines to become the ultimate guitar player!

-The Ultimate Guitar Arpeggio Book-

With this book we are looking at arpeggio shapes starting from the most basic triad arpeggios to the more advanced extended arpeggios such as ninths, elevenths and thirteenths. So many arpeggio books I have read in the past have hundreds of unnecessary shapes that are just repeated in every key. This can be confusing and make players think they have a massive volume of arpeggio shapes to learn, which they don't.

-The Ultimate Guitar Pentatonic Scales Book (Volume One)-

The idea of volume one is that by the end of it you won't just be playing up and down the five 2NPS pentatonic boxes aimlessly. You should have developed a musical purpose and understand the importance of knowing the intervals, where the root notes are and how to move around the guitar neck freely in any key you desire.

-The Ultimate Guitar Pentatonic Scales Book (Volume Two)-

Moving onto more advanced concepts and ideas using 3NPS pentatonic shapes and embedded arpeggios within the major and minor pentatonic scale. This book is aimed at the intermediate to advanced players.

-The Ultimate Guitar Major Modes Book-

Learn how to write your own modal licks and songs with the seven modes of the major scale. This book dives deep into each of the seven modes explaining what they are, what scales systems to use, arpeggios, chords and so much more. Learn over 70 modal rock licks to spice up your playing.

-The Ultimate Guitar Sweep Picking Book-

Sweep picking can be one of the most daunting techniques to learn and play and speaking from experience I understand the frustrations of not knowing what shapes are best to learn and play! This book gives you all the tools you need to understand how to build your own sweep picking licks and become a master of the sweeps in no time! Jumping straight to the juicy bits focusing on arpeggio shapes specifically for sweep picking that loop in bars of 4/4 and are movable to any key! Whether new to sweep picking or a more advanced player this book is the ultimate sweep picking reference book for inspiration.

www.karlgolden.org/books

Tag me on Instagram with your progress **www.instagram.com/karlgolden**
Also check out **www.karlgolden.org/YouTube** for some fun free guitar lessons with tabs including my classic **'100 Riffs'** and **'Top 10 Riffs'**. These medley videos are a great way to learn lots of different riffs on the guitar and remember them!

GUITAR TABS GLOSSARY

TABLATURE (TABS) EXPLAINED

Tablature illustrates the six strings on the guitar. Notes and chords are represented by the placement of fret numbers on each given string(s).

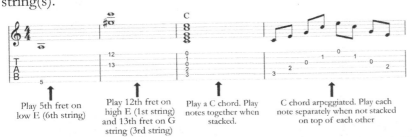

Play 5th fret on low E (6th string)

Play 12th fret on high E (1st string) and 13th fret on G string (3rd string)

Play a C chord. Play notes together when stacked.

C chord arpeggiated. Play each note separately when not stacked on top of each other

BENDING NOTES

SLIGHT BEND

Play the note and bend it slightly to the equivalent of half a fret.

HALF STEP

Play the note and bend string one half step. Equivalent of one fret.

WHOLE STEP

Play the note and bend string one whole step. Equivalent of two frets.

WHOLE STEP & A HALF

Play the note and bend string whole step and a half. Equivalent of three frets.

TWO STEPS

Play the note and bend string two whole steps. Equivalent of four frets.

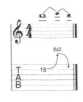

BEND AND RELEASE

Play the note and bend it then release back down to the original note.

PREBEND

Bend the string to specific note and then pick note.

PREBEND AND RELEASE

Bend the string, play it, then release to the original note.

PREBEND AND BEND

Bend the string, play it, then bend to next note.

A half step is the smallest interval in western music which is equal to one fret. A whole step equals two frets.

BENDS INVOLVING MORE THAN ONE STRING

Play the note and bend the string while playing additional note(s) on other strings

UNISON BENDS

Play both notes and immediately bend the lower note to the same pitch as the higher note.

DOUBLE NOTE BENDS

Play both notes and immediately bend both strings simultaneously.

BENDS WITH STATIONARY NOTES

Play notes and bend lower pitch, then hold until released back to original note.

HARMONICS

NATURAL HARMONICS

A finger of the fretting hand lightly touches the note or notes indicated in the ta and then picked. Place finger just over the fret to get best sound.

ARTIFICIAL HARMONICS

The first tab number is fretted then the pic hand produces the harmonic by using a finger to touch lightly the same stri in the second tab in brackets and then picke with another finger.

PINCHED HARMONICS

The first note is fretted then the pick han produces the harmonics by squeezing the pick firmly while using the tip of the index finger in the pick attack. The note i the brackets is the pitch that should be created.

TAPPED HARMONICS

The first tab number is fretted then the pic hand produces the harmonic by using a finger to tap on the note in the brack

ARTICULATIONS

HAMMER ON

Play lower note, then "hammer on" to higher note with another finger. Only the first note is picked.

PULL OFF

Play higher note, then "pull off" to lower note with another finger. Only the first note is picked.

HAMMER ON FROM NOWHERE

Hammer on first note (T) with fretting hand. No picking used with hammer ons from nowhere.

FINGER TAPPING

Not to be confused with the hammer on from nowhere this uses a finger from the picking hand to tap the note indicated with the 'T' and then pull off to the next notes held by the fretting hand.

SLAP & POP

Use your thumb of your picking hand to hit down or 'slap' the note in the tabs (s). Use your index finger of your picking hand to pluck or 'pop' the note in the tab (p).

LEFT HAND FINGERING

This indicates which fingers to use with your fretting hand.
1 = Index
2 = Middle
3 = Ring Finger
4 = Pinky
T = Thumb
0 = No fingers!

LEGATO SLIDE

Play note and slide to the next note. Only the first note is picked.

WAH WAH PEDAL

'O' means to close your wah (foot up) and '+' means to open your wah (foot down)

TREMOLO PICKING

The note or notes are picked as fast as possible using alternate picking.

VIBRATO

The pitch of a note is alliterated slightly by a rapid shaking of the fretting hand finger. Can be vertical, horizontal or circular vibrato.

DOWN & UP STROKES

Notes or chords are to be played with either a:
⊓ = Downstroke
V = Upstroke

RIGHT HAND FINGERING

This indicates which fingers to use with your picking hand
p = Thumb
i = Index
m = Middle
a = Ring Finger
c = Pinky

MUTED STRINGS

A percussive sound is made by laying the fretting hand across all six strings while your picking hand strikes the specific strings in tabs.

PALM MUTE

The note or notes are muted by the palm of the picking hand by lightly touching the strings near the bridge of the guitar,

TRILL

Hammer on and pull off consecutively and as fast as possible between the original note and the grace note.

ACCENT

Notes or chords are to be played with added emphasis.

STACCATO

Notes or chords are to be played roughly half their value and with separation.

VOLUME SWELLS

Turn the volume knob down on your guitar then play the note in tab and quickly turn up your guitar volume and then turn back down creating volume swells.

145

Made in the USA
Las Vegas, NV
29 August 2023